D1566156

Textual Politics and the Language Poets

GEORGE HARTLEY

Textual Politics ███████
███████ and the Language Poets

INDIANA UNIVERSITY PRESS

Bloomington and Indianapolis

Chapters from this book also appear in *Poetics Journal* and *boundary 2*.

"White Roses," *Selected Poems* by John Ashbery. © 1985 by John Ashbery. All rights reserved. Reprinted by permission of Viking Penguin, a division of Penguin Books USA, Inc.

Excerpts from *Imaginations* by William Carlos Williams © 1970 by Florence H. Williams, used by permission of New Directions Publishing Corporation.

© 1989 by George Hartley

All rights reserved

No part of this book may be reproduced or utilized in any form or by any means, electronic or mechanical, including photocopying and recording, or by any information storage and retrieval system, without permission in writing from the publisher. The Association of American University Presses' Resolution on Permissions constitutes the only exception to this prohibition.

Manufactured in the United States of America

Library of Congress Cataloging-in-Publication Data

Hartley, George.
    Textual politics and the language poets.

    Bibliography: p.
    Includes index.
    1. American poetry—20th century—History and
criticism.   2. Language and languages in literature.
3. Poetics.   I. Title.
PS310.L33H37   1989   811'.54'09   88-46024
ISBN 0-253-32716-4

1 2 3 4 5 93 92 91 90 89

to Jennifer, Katy, and Dylan

CONTENTS

Acknowledgments   *ix*

Preface   *xi*

ONE   **"endless PROTEANL inkages": Language Poetry and the Avant-Garde Tradition**   **1**

TWO   **Ideological Struggle and the Possibility of an Oppositional Poetic Practice**   **26**

THREE   **Jameson's Perelman: Reification and the Material Signifier**   **42**

FOUR   **Realism and Reification: The Poetics and Politics of Three Language Poets**   **53**

FIVE   **Praxis and Syntaxis: Ideology and the Economy of Space**   **76**

Works Cited   *101*

Index   *107*

Acknowledgments

I wish to thank all those people who made this book possible: Jennifer and Katy Hartley; my committee members: Lee Bartlett, Michael Fischer, George Huaco, and Hugh Witemeyer; the many poets who provided me with invaluable material and advice: Bruce Andrews, David Benedetti, Steve Benson, Charles Bernstein, David Bromige, Clark Coolidge, Robert Grenier, Carla Harryman, Lyn Hejinian, Susan Howe, Douglas Messerli, Michael Palmer, Bob Perelman, Nick Piombino, Kit Robinson, James Sherry, Ron Silliman, and Barrett Watten; the UNM Graduate Students Association for their Student Research Grant; all friends and family members who have seen me through years of graduate study; my mother and father, who taught me the value of education; and Grant Keener, who taught me how to read.

Preface

"Let us undermine the bourgeoisie." So Ron Silliman ends his contribution to "The Politics of Poetry" symposium in *L=A=N=G=U=A=G=E* 9/10 (October 1979). The organizing topic of that symposium was "what qualities writing has or could have that contribute to an understanding or critique of society, seen as a capitalist system." While many respondents pointed out their difficulty with the notion that writing *per se* has any generalizable qualities, most of the participants agreed that, in one way or another, a particular poetry at a particular time may offer a critique of bourgeois society. Specifically, what has come to be known as Language Poetry is held out to be one of the poetic modes of the present moment (in addition to certain minority, feminist, and gay poetries) which functions as such a critique.

But in what ways can the following excerpt from Charles Bernstein's "Lift Plow Plates" be seen as a critique of capitalist society?

> For brief scratches, omits,
> lays away the oars (hours).
> Flagrant immersion besets all
> the best boats. Hands, hearts
> don't slip, solidly
> (sadly) departs.

> *(Islets/Irritations 9)*

In what ways is this writing " 'decentered', 'community controlled', taken out of the *service* of the capitalist project," as Bernstein himself puts it in his contribution to "The Politics of Poetry?" This book is a critical analysis of how some so-called Language Poets have answered those questions.

Who are the Language poets? The answer to that question depends on how one defines the label. One could begin, for instance, by listing those poets (most born between 1940 and 1950) who for fifteen years or so have appeared in the following Language anthologies: *Toothpick, Lisbon & the Orcas Islands* (1973); *Alcheringa* (1975); *Open Letter* (1977); *Hills* (1980); *Ironwood* (1982); *Paris Review* (1982); *The L=A=N=G=U=A=G=E Book* (1984); *Change* (1985); *Writing/Talks* (1985); *boundary 2* (1986); *In the American Tree* (1986); and *"Language" Poetries* (1987). While the periphery of the group remains rather amorphous—Silliman lists almost eighty poets who might have accompanied the forty who are represented in *In the American Tree*—many names frequently recur in anthologies, critical essays, and poetry magazines such as *This, Tottel's, Roof, Hills, Miam, Qu, L=A=N=G=U=A=G=E, The Difficulties, A Hundred Posters,* and more recently (though not as the predominant group) *Sulfur, Temblor, Sink,* and *Tramen.* Those frequent names are Bruce Andrews, Rae Armantrout, Steve Benson, Charles Bernstein, David Bromige, Clark Coolidge, Alan Davies, Ray DiPalma, Robert Grenier, Carla Harryman, Lyn Hejinian, Susan Howe, Steve McCaffery, Michael Palmer,

Bob Perelman, Kit Robinson, Peter Seaton, James Sherry, Ron Silliman, Diane Ward, Barrett Watten, and Hannah Weiner.

Why the name Language? The answer to that question would take us beyond the above listing of names—for what poet in one way or another does *not* deal with language? What particular use of or attitude towards language connects these poets and excludes others? Before proceding with that analysis, I need to point out what I am *not* doing in the pages that follow. I do not attempt to define that which most of the poets I discuss have denounced—the label Language Poetry itself. As Silliman has argued, at least since his editing of "The Dwelling Place: 9 Poets," what connects these writers (first called "language-centered" in Steve McCaffery's 1976 essay, "The Death of the Subject") is not any particular style or practice but a "community of concern for language as the center of whatever activity poems might be" (*Alcheringa*, 118). The way Susan Howe, for instance, enacts this concern with the foregrounding of language does not at all resemble the way Silliman often does. While some of Howe's poems might superficially resemble some of Bruce Andrews's, the tone of each could hardly be more dissimilar (as we shall see).

Nevertheless, one can generalize more safely about the poetic concerns which have led these poets, from the first issue of *This* in 1971 to the present, to establish an elaborate network of small presses and talk series, a network which has possibly allowed for a greater degree of cross-fertilization and of independence from the defining process of academic criticism than perhaps any group since the Black Mountain school. Those concerns, for the most part, grow out of the rejection of the dominant model for poetic production and reception today—the so-called voice poem. According to many Language poets, the voice poem depends on a model of communication that needs to be challenged: the notion that the poet (a self-present subject) transmits a particular message ("experience," "emotion") to a reader (another self-present subject) through a language which is neutral, transparent, "natural." Carla Harryman's "For She" can be read as an exploration of narrative assumptions:

> The back of the head resting on the pillow was not wasted. We couldn't hear each other speak. The puddle in the bathroom, the sassy one. There were many years between us. I stared the stranger into facing up to Maxine, who had come out of the forest bad from wet nights. I came from an odd bed, a vermilion riot attracted to loud dogs. Nonetheless, I could pay my rent and provide for him. On this occasion she apologized.
>
> *(Under the Bridge)*

Harryman's poem goes through the motions of narrative, but one would be hard put to summarize what story has been told. "For She" challenges the "naturalness" of the narrative mode by foregrounding the devices which organize otherwise disparate elements into a seemingly seamless whole. This challenge to the "natural" look of the voice poem is one major concern of most Language poets.

Bernstein writes that "there is no natural writing style" (*The L=A=N=G=U=A=G=E Book,* 43; hereafter cited as *LB*). What looks natural about a given poem is actually the result of a number of procedures and assumptions about writing that the author may be more or less conscious of when composing. Those procedures and assumptions are in fact social constructions which have become conventions. Thus most Language poets attempt to remind us of the socially contrived basis of any writing. They do not do so, however, by abandoning modes of writing, for such an action is impossible. "Modes cannot be escaped," Bernstein continues, "but they can be taken for granted. They can also be meant" (p. 44). It is the mode-that-is-meant, so to speak, the exploration of the possibilities for meaning-production, which lies behind most Language poetry.

The last point cannot be stressed enough. For, although these poets rigorously deconstruct the notions behind much contemporary poetry in this country, that deconstruction is often followed by an attempt to develop a constructive writing practice. As poet Steve Benson has put it, these writers "markedly propose conscious value to what could otherwise be taken as impingements in a literature of autonomous display" (*In the American Tree,* 487). Such writing is seen to be constructive in its demolition of the conventional relationship between the active (dictatorial) writer and the passive (victimized) reader. Language writing is often posed as an attempt to draw the reader into the production process by leaving the connections between various elements open, thus allowing the reader to produce the connections between those elements. In this way, presumably, the reader recognizes his or her part in the social process of production. But just as important, the ambiguity of the structure of many of these poems should remind the reader that any connections drawn are arbitrary. It is the framing process itself, and by extension the process of ideological framing, which is no longer taken for granted. I refer to this laying bare of the framing process as "syntaxis." Through this dissection, the exploration of the possibilities of syntactical construction serves as an ideology critique by drawing our attention to the socially-determined frames by which we constitute our world.

In the pages that follow I explore the claims and writings that have led to and support such a process of syntaxis. In order to emphasize that the formal dimension of these poems does not in itself produce a radical critique of bourgeois ideology, I trace in chapter one the recent history of formal concerns in the works of Emily Dickinson, Gertrude Stein, William Carlos Williams, the Russian Futurist poets, the Dadaists, André Breton, Louis Zukofsky, Charles Olson, and John Ashbery. I stress that whatever political value might be attached to a given poetic mode must take into account the historical context in which each manifestation of that mode appears. While Susan Howe, for example, may model her own work on certain aspects of Dickinson's, one must always keep in mind the century that separates the two. No mode, in other words, does its work all by itself in some transhistorical way (as Julia Kristeva's notion of revolution in poetic language might lead one to conclude).

In chapter two I begin an analysis of the political claims that various Language poets have made for their writing. What do Ron Silliman and Steve McCaffery mean, for instance, when they claim that their work is a challenge to reification in capitalist society? How can such poetry be seen as a challenge to the notion of the self-present subject which is seen to underlie capitalist ideology? And how do these poets see their work as the creation of a democratic writer-reader relationship rather than as an obliteration of any possibility whatsoever to read such work? I also propose a reading of Louis Althusser's theory of ideology that provides theoretical and political support for such a poetic practice.

In chapter three I focus on a Marxist challenge to the claims of some Language poets, in particular, Fredric Jameson's implied charge that such poetry, in that it resembles schizophrenic language as Lacan has described it, contributes to—rather than challenges—the reification of late capitalist society. Because of Jameson's influence on the theoretical development of many Language poets, such a confrontation promises a fruitful exploration of the political claims of the poets in this study.

I extend that confrontation in chapter four by focusing in detail on the argument of some Language poets that literary realism is a form of reification. Since the Jameson-"Language" school debate so closely resembles the earlier Lukács-Frankfurt School debate, and since many Language writers draw on the aesthetic theory of members of the Frankfurt School, I summarize the major points of that earlier debate. As the Marxist interpretation of the word "reification" comes from Lukács, such a review is especially important for clarifying the issues of the present writers.

The realism-equals-reification argument, which I explore in chapter four, is predominantly a negative argument in that it remains within the categories of the view it seeks to displace. To the extent that Language writers see their work as a denial of reference, they remain within a referential frame. But in chapter five I point out that the shift from a referential to a syntactical frame—or, as I explain, from a paradigmatic to a syntagmatic frame—provides a truly constructive context in which to view the political claims of some Language poets. Because such an argument depends to a certain degree on notions of syntax developed by the minimalist and conceptualist artists of the 1960s and early 1970s, I review the arguments of those artists and show how those concerns tie in with Language poetry. Chapter five also serves as a conclusion, for it is in the turn to what I have called syntax that many of the concerns which I explore in the earlier chapters come together as a rigorous critique of ideology.

I wish to stress at this point that there is no single argument, political or otherwise, that applies to everyone labeled a "Language poet." I make no claim, therefore, that the particular political positions to be analyzed in the following pages apply to all or even most of the Language poets. As should become clear, even the handful of poets whom I discuss here vary widely in their view of the connections between poetry and politics. To the extent that a particular point may seem applicable to all whom I discuss here, then some of these claims are more generalizable than others, and it has been my goal to make clear which claims can and cannot be extended beyond a particular poet. Because of this difficulty, I have tended to focus on those Language poets who have made specifically Marxist claims for their work. Those poets are the San Francisco Bay area poets Ron Silliman (author of *Ketjak* [1978], *Tjanting* [1981], *ABC* [1983], *The Age of Huts* [1986]; and editor of *In the American Tree* [1986]), Bob Perelman (*7 Works* [1978], *Primer* [1981], *The First World* [1986]; editor of *Hills* magazine and *Writing/Talks* [1985]), and Barrett Watten (*Opera-Works* [1975], *1–10* [1980], *Total Syntax* [1985], *Progress* [1986]; co-editor [with Robert Grenier] of *This* magazine, co-editor [with Lyn Hejinian] of *Poetics Journal*), the New York poets Charles Bernstein (*Poetic Justice* [1979], *Controlling Intersts* [1980], *Islets/Irritations* [1983], *Content's Dream* [1986], *The Sophist* [1987]; co-editor [with Bruce Andrews] of *L=A=N=G=U=A=G=E* magazine and *The L=A=N=G=U=A=G=E Book* [1984]) and Bruce Andrews (*Praxis* [1978], *Sonnets—memento mori* [1980], *Wobbling* [1980], *Love Songs* [1982], *Give Em Enough Rope* [1985]; co-editor [with Charles Bernstein] of *L=A=N=G=U=A=G=E* magazine and *The L=A=N=G=U=A=G=E Book* [1984]), and Toronto poet Steve McCaffery (whose work has been primarily performance and sound poetry; editor of *The Politics of the Referent* [*Open Letter* 1977]).

When I choose other poets as examples, I mean for them to be viewed as examples of the particular point I am making at the time, not as poets who would share fully the arguments of the six poets above. Some poets, such as Clark Coolidge and Robert Grenier, disavow any Marxist claims whatsoever. Steven Benson, while not denying certain political intentions, chooses a much more cautious relationship to Marxism, especially to what he sees as its tendency towards an either/or logic. Thus any claims that Language poetry in general is a Marxist challenge to bourgeois poetics is an illegitimate overgeneralization. The six poets I study in depth in the final chapters, however, all in one way or another see the syntactical play in their poetry as a socialist critique of the ideology of capitalism.

Textual Politics and the Language Poets

"endless PROTEANL inkages"

Language Poetry and
the Avant-Garde Tradition

I begin this essay with an apparent oxymoron: avant-garde tradition. As art critic Rosalind Krauss explains in her essay "The Originality of the Avant-Garde," one of the key myths of early twentieth-century avant-garde art is its original status, its supposed separation from the "corrupt" tradition (or "institution" as critic Peter Bürger puts it) of art. But Krauss goes on to claim that the avant-garde work—like all works of art—is always already a copy. It is a copy in two senses: (1) it copies formal techniques that can always be found in previous works, and (2) it copies what is already a copy, one code signifying not a referent "in the world" but another code or trope. The supposed original, in other words, is already a repetition.

Whether or not the avant-garde can be characterized by its reputed valorization of the original—Duchamp's ready-mades at the very least complicate such an attribution—Krauss's repudiation of the concept of originality dispenses with the related notion that there cannot be an avant-garde tradition. The vanguard, then, can be seen as made up not by those who have new ideas but by those who challenge their time's hegemonic conceptualization of art.

More specifically, however, we can identify certain techniques, concepts, and social stances as characteristic of the avant-garde of the late nineteenth and the twentieth centuries. The technical emphasis of this period is the foregrounding of the aesthetic medium, which for poetry predominantly means the self-reflexive use of language. The period's conceptual emphasis, beginning roughly with the artistic appropriation of Walter Pater's impressionism, has tended to be the relativist challenge to empiricist notions of perception and representation. And its social stance has generally been anti-bourgeois, anti-establishment, anti-institutional, and anti-commercial, a stance often but not always associated with leftist politics—some notable exceptions being Ezra Pound and the Italian Futurists.

I will begin with a qualified definition of avant-garde in order to dispense with the possible misapprehension that what has come to be called Language poetry is something radically new. Certainly when contrasted with much of American verse written in the past twenty years or so, such as that which appears in *American Poetry Review* (a verse which poses the poem as the expression of a significant and often personal experience of the individual poet), then Language poetry might appear quite new. And one might argue that the particular concerns of many Language poets—such as the question of reference, of the bourgeois monadic subject, and of the role of language (and ideology) in constituting our experience—are fairly recent concerns growing out of the structuralist intervention in the human sciences since the 1950s.

But most of the poets I will discuss insist on seeing their work as a continuation of the American modernist project, as the title of Ron Silliman's recent anthology of Language poetry, *In the American Tree,* suggests. The formal qualities which I will treat in this chapter, though not common among other poets today, have a rich century-long tradition.

By "tradition," however, I do not mean to imply some teleological unfolding of lines of aesthetic kinship, as would be behind a statement such as "Language poet Bruce Andrews is the direct heir of Russian Futurist poet Velimir Khlebnikov." What I *do* mean by the word "tradition" is a roughly similar set of concerns and techniques, a general self-conscious positioning of the artists against the dominant aesthetic assumptions of their day. In other words, I reject the impulse to try to establish a direct line of influence, but I do see the need for recognizing certain formal, conceptual, and/or political similarities between the writers who have come to be called Language poets and particular poets of the past, such as Gertrude Stein, William Carlos Williams, Vladimir Mayakovsky, André Breton, Tristan Tzara, Charles Olson, and John Ashbery. Only by recognizing such similarities can we then attempt to see the specific historical differences between poets of different periods. Only then can we attempt to determine the interplay of formal qualities and historical contexts. For although we may see formal similarities between certain Russian Futurist poets and certain Language poets, we must also take into account the social contexts of each—the Russian Revolution for the former, and the post-Vietnam, post-Watergate age of capitalist recession for the latter.

In light of all this, my first example of an important precursor may seem odd, since she has hardly, until recently, been associated with avant-garde aesthetics or oppositional politics. Besides Walt Whitman, however, Emily Dickinson stands out as American poetry's first major formal innovator. In particular, Susan Howe—a writer who, though hating the label, is often associated with Language poetry—sees Dickinson as a major precursor of her own work. Such a connection between the two is not readily apparent; but Howe explains her indebtedness to Dickinson in her recent study, *My Emily Dickinson.* In discussing "My Life had stood—a Loaded Gun," Howe writes:

> for Emily Dickinson, who was geographically separated from European custom, the past, that sovereign source, must break poetic structure open for future absorption of words and definition. . . .[She] adopted parataxis and rupture to tell the feverish haste, the loss, to warn of storm approaching [the Civil War]—Brute force, mechanism. Cassandra was a woman. All power, including the power of Love, all nature, including the nature of Time, is utterly unstable. (p. 116)

Even though Dickinson's work is written "in the plain style of puritan literary tradition [and] there are no complications of phrasing," Howe points out that "Each word is deceptively simple, deceptively easy to define. But definition seeing rather than perceiving, hearing and not understanding, is only the shadow of meaning. Like all poems on the trace of the holy, this one [above] remains outside the protection of specific solution" (p. 35). Howe's description of Dickinson's work not surprisingly describes her own as well: attraction to the past; breaking of poetic form; absorption of words and definitions; parataxis; rupture; concern with women and power and instability; and disdain for the protection of specific solution. These features can be seen in the following poem from *Defenestration of Prague:*

Transgression links remembering
Dark spell

terror   Ideal
(spangs like stars)

Winter
a wound to the sun

empty desolation of mortality

Old age of winter
(lean pallor

bone ghost)
plunder and massacre

Florimell embarks blindly
(being lost)

to interpret the world

chivalric courtesy
chivalric constancy

quelled liturgy
(double sense softly)

illusory sanctuary of memory

Seven men suggest an army
furious humor of cruelty

Fantasticality
nimble phantasma capering on a page

with antic gesture

(p. 29)

Being the sixth poem of the second section of the book, this poem, like most of Howe's works, stands both as a part of a series and as a discrete unit. Such is the case with the positioning of the words within the poem, each connected to each with only a hint at syntax. The words and phrases skate around the object of the poem, providing brief flashes and suggestions of context, but giving no clear picture of what we are reading about and no clear sense of distinct compound units of words. Such syntactical indeterminacy— due to the lack of punctuation other than parenthesis, the complicated enjambment, and the ambiguous capitalization of words—resists the totalization and hierarchy of the sentence, an indeterminacy which can be seen both as a political and an epistemological analogy to the book's theme. The Defenestration of Prague, Howe has explained in correspondence, "was the violent event that ushered in the Thirty Years War. . . . This Defenestration marked the end of a dream for some kind unity between science, mysticism, and art." It also marked the return of the violent papal repression of difference and controversy, the stamping out of artistic, intellectual, and spiritual freedom.

For Howe the opening up of syntax is the opening up of thought, the denial of imposed intellectual categories. "Emily Dickinson and Gertrude Stein," Howe writes, ". . . conducted a skillful and ironic investigation of patriarchal authority over literary history. Who polices questions of grammar, parts of speech, connection, and connotation? Whose order is shut inside the structure of the sentence?" (*My Emily Dickinson*, 11). What is needed is a new grammar: "Fantasticality/ nimble phantasma capering on a page// with antic gesture."

Stein's work, as Howe suggests, is a second major precursor of Language poetry. The December 1978 issue of $L=A=N=G=U=A=G=E$ (the journal, edited by Bruce Andrews and Charles Bernstein, which served as a forum for poets involved with so-called language-writing) began with a special feature on readings of Stein's *Tender Buttons* (1914). A key passage from these readings is the first poem in Stein's work:

A CARAFE, THAT IS A BLIND GLASS

A kind in glass and a cousin, a spectacle and nothing strange a single hurt color and an arrangement in a system to pointing. All this and not ordinary, not unordered in not resembling. The difference is spreading.

Before attempting to analyze the significance of this poem for many of the Language poets, I want to quote extensively from certain readings by the poets themselves. Michael Davidson writes:

[Most critics] operate on either side of a referential paradigm; one wants her to mean nothing and the other wants her to mean intrinsically. But what makes *Tender Buttons* so vital is not the strategies by which meaning is avoided or encoded but how each piece points at possibilities for meaning. Unlike the Symbolist who creates beautiful detachable artifacts, Stein's prose is firmly tied to the world—but it is a world constantly under construction, a world in which the equation of word and thing can no longer be taken for granted. "The difference is spreading" not only foreshadows deconstructive thought; it recognizes that between one term (a carafe) and a possible substitute (a blind glass) exists a barrier, not an equal sign, and it is this difference which supports all signification.

From Jackson Mac Low (a fellow traveler and precursor of much in Language poetry):

> But can I specify anything beyond sounds? To use a phrase I first heard from Spencer Holst, it gives "the sensation of meaning," but can I connect the meanings of the words as readily as I find their sounds connected?
> Beyond the obvious fact that the carafe is made of glass I can see only certain connections of meanings.

From Robert Grenier:

> It's not "snapshorts" (moves; don't copy nature), & it's not "the pathetic fallacy" (though it includes much of the artist's process). And it ain't "abstract."

While each of these poets approaches the poem differently, a general consensus does seem to emerge. Stein's importance for them appears to lie in the following qualities of her work:

1. Although her work *appears* to be meaningless, it does have meaning; in fact, it seems to be an exploration of the very conditions for meaning.

2. Meaning is not forwarded as something existing out in the world but as an interaction between subject and object.

3. Her work appears to operate under the assumptions of the Saussurean conception of meaning as a function of a system of difference.

4. She does not write in order to enclose (define, delimit, decipher) the world but to move within it; in other words, she does not function according to the static determinism of the noun but through the process of relationship.

5. Her foregrounding of the material side of language (sound, rhythm, syntax) is a formal analogy of the process of perception—the "movement 'spreading' from transparency . . . to the implied darkness & opacity of blindness."

Language poet Lyn Hejinian argues in *Temblor* 3 (1986) that Stein's language is not only meaningful but is in fact a form of realism superior to what we customarily call realism, a mimesis not of the external object but of the perceptual process, a realism not of subject matter but of artistic means. Stein offers a later generation of poets a way of making sense of the way we make sense.

As Robert Grenier goes on to point out in his $L=A=N=G=U=A=G=E$ essay, however, Stein's other work may not offer itself so readily as a model for the Language school:

... I think it's at best a "creative misreading" of Stein to take her work as a whole as a primary instance of "language-oriented writing."...([Her other works], if anything, a prototype of confessional poetry) all are intent to make new ways to say something—show her thinking language not as object-in-itself, but as composition functioning in the composition of the world.

In other words, while there may be formal similarities between *Tender Buttons* and some Language poetry, Grenier claims that there is also a significant difference in their aims for poetry.

The attraction of *Tender Buttons* for poet Ron Silliman lies in Stein's use of the sentence rather than the line as the unit of composition. The sentences in Stein's portraits of homely objects are juxtaposed so as to create friction, like the units of perspective are in a Cubist painting. In standard prose, sentences are arranged within the paragraph in syllogistic order, one premise contributing logically to the preceding and succeeding ones. But Stein's sentence arrangement challenges our syllogistic expectations. "The syllogistic move above the sentence level to an exterior reference is possible," Silliman writes, "but the nature of the book reverses the direction of this movement. Rather than making the shift in an automatic and gestalt sort of way, the reader is forced to deduce it from the partial views and associations posited in each sentence" (*The New Sentence*, 84).

Tender Buttons thus presages the "New Sentence," Silliman's term for contemporary prose poetry of the type that he and his associates often write. Silliman characterizes the "New Sentence" as follows:

1) The paragraph (rather than the stanza) organizes the sentences;
2) The paragraph is a unit of quantity, not logic or argument;
3) Sentence length (rather than the line) is a unit of measure;
4) Sentence structure is altered for torque, or increased polysemy/ambiguity;
5) Syllogistic movement is (a) limited; (b) controlled;
6) Primary syllogistic movement is between the preceding and following sentences;
7) Secondary syllogistic movement is toward the paragraph as a whole, or the total work;
8) The limiting of syllogistic movement keeps the reader's attention at or very close to the level of language, the sentence level or below. (*The New Sentence*, p. 91)

Here is an example from his *Tjanting* (1981):

Forcing oneself to it. It wld've been new with a blue pen. Giving oneself to it. Of about to within which what without. Hands writing. Out of the rockpile grew poppies. Sip mineral water, smoke cigar. Again I began. One sees seams. These clouds break up in the late afternoon, blue patches. I began again but it was not beginning. Somber hue of gray day sky filled the yellow room. Ridges & bridges. Each sentence accounts for all the rest. I was I discovered on the road. Not this. Counting my fingers to get different answers. Four wooden chairs in the yard, rain-warpd, wind-blown. Cat on the bear rug naps. Grease sizzles & spits on the stove top. In paradise plane wrecks are distributed evenly throughout the desert. All the same, no difference, no blame. Moon's rise at noon. In the air hung odor of ammonia. I felt disease. Not not not-this. Reddest red contains trace of blue. That to the this then. What words tear out. All elements fit into nine crystal structures. Waiting for the cheese to go blue. Thirty-two. Measure meters pause. Applause. (p. 12)

What makes this an example of the "New Sentence" is not the nature of the sentences themselves—even though some of them do stand out because of their nonstandard diction or syntax—but the arrangement of the individual sentences within the paragraph and within the poem as a whole (which is 213 pages long). Despite its inverted syntax, "Out of the rock pile grew poppies," for instance, is a fairly ordinary referential sentence. Coming right after "Hands writing," however, this sentence seems to demand to be encapsulated between quotation marks, to be presented as an example of what hands write rather than as a direct statement to be taken at face value. "Rockpile" is then metonymically recalled in the following sentence in "mineral water," while the self-conscious attention to usually rote actions, sipping and smoking, refers back to "Hands writing." Not much later our rockpile sentence becomes recontextualized even further by "One sees seams," which refers in part to the reader's perception of Silliman's writing process itself—the deliberate focusing of attention on the contextualizing process of writing—the rockpile now becoming a trope for the pile of sentences which is *Tjanting,* out of which, despite superficial appearances, meaning coheres and accretes. The gaps between sentences (the locus of tension or "torque"), the visible seams, here take the place of the line break and draw our attention to the materiality of the words as words, not simply as transparent signifiers.

Such writing is reminiscent not only of Stein but of William Carlos Williams as well, especially his *Kora in Hell* (1918). Influenced as Stein was by the European avant-garde painters, particularly the Cubists and the Dadaists, Williams writes words and sentences that continually drift between materiality and transparency. The following paragraph from *Kora in Hell* illustrates the "torquing" of sentences that Silliman values:

How smoothly the car runs. This must be the road. Queer how a road juts in. How the dark catches among those trees! How the light clings to the canal! Yes, there's one table taken, we'll not be alone. This place has possibilities. Will you bring *her* here? Perhaps—and when we meet on the stair, shall we speak, say it is some acquaintance—or pass silent? Well, a jest's a jest but how poor this tea is. Think of a life in this place, here in these hills by these truck farms. Whose life? Why there, back of you. If a woman laughs a little loudly one always thinks that way of her. But how she bedizens the country-side. Quite an old world glamour. If it were not for—but one cannot have everything. What poor tea it was. How cold it's grown. Cheering, a light is that way among the trees. That heavy laugh! How it will rattle these branches in six weeks' time. (*Imaginations,* 37)

One immediate difference between this and the Silliman passage is that here one can imagine a narrative unity—a person in the country riding by the place he may take his lover and remembering a past rendezvous when the tea wasn't very good. This particular passage from *Kora*, in other words, could be read as stream of consciousness. Nevertheless, the reader's need to bridge the significant gaps between the sentences and the resulting lack of a narrative frame provide Silliman with a model for his own work. Besides the tension between the sentences, Williams's work also presages Silliman's in its attention to detail (much like James Joyce's portrait of Leopold Bloom's world). In his prologue to *Kora* Williams discusses his attention to detail:

> The true value is that peculiarity which gives an object a character by itself. The associational or sentimental value is the false. Its imposition is due to lack of imagination, to an easy lateral sliding. The attention has been held too rigid on the one plane instead of following a more flexible, jagged resort. It is to loosen the attention, my attention since I occupy part of the field, that I write these improvisations. (p. 14)

In order to frustrate such "easy lateral sliding," Williams assembles a mass of discrete details without the usual "associational or sentimental value," details such as the condition of the road, the light and dark, the activity of surrounding people, the quality of the tea, and the weather. Silliman in turn draws our attention to the poet's pen in motion, the rockpile and poppies, the mineral water and cigar, the gray sky in the yellow room, and so on. By accumulating such details in *Tjanting* Silliman draws a portrait of the daily life of a poet in San Francisco in the late 1970s-early 1980s.

Such is not the case with all of his work, however. Consider the following passage from "Rhizome":

> Proliferation of the alphabet world.
>   Poured
> of truck, turned of oranges.
>   Mushroom out of which
> cloud rose.
>   Experience is predicated on exist-
> ence.
>   Goals we have, should not poems.
>   A bird
> I casual conversation into tree.
>   He wall of us
> turned in the his fud.
>
>   (*The Age of Huts*, 79)

Here the focus is not on fragmented referential details but on what Russian Futurist poets Velimir Khlebnikov and Alexei Kruchonykh called "the word as such." In the 1913 manifesto by that name, Khlebnikov and Kruchonykh characterized their own work as an art in which "the word was developed as itself alone" (*The King of Time*, 119), as can be seen in Khlebnikov's "Incantation by Laughter," which I quote both in transliterated Russian and in English in order to provide the rhyme and rhythm plays of the original:

ZAKLYATIE SMEKHOM
   O, rassmeites', smekhachi!
   O, zasmeites', smekhachi!
Chto smeyutsya smekhami, chto smeyanstvuyut smeyal' no.
   O, zasmeites' usmeyal' no!
O, rassmeshishch nadsmeyal' nykh—smekh usmeinykh smekhachei!
O, issmeisya rassmeyal' no, smekh nadsmeinykh smeyachei!
   Smeievo, smeievo,
   Usmei, osmei, smeshiki, smeshiki,
      Smeyunchiki, smeyunchiki,
   O, rassmeites', smekhachi!
   O, zasmeites', smekhachi!

                                      (Kern, 61)

INCANTATION BY LAUGHTER
   O laugh it out, you laughsters!
   O laugh it up, you laughsters!
So they laugh with laughters, so they laugherize delaughly.
   O laugh it up belaughably!
O the laughingstock of the laughed-upon—the laugh of
                              belaughed laughsters!
O laugh it out roundlaughingly, the laugh of laughed-at
                                 laughians!
   Laugherino, laugherino,
   Laughify, laughicate, laugholets, laugholets,
      Laughikins, laughikins,
   O laugh it out, you laughsters!
   O laugh it up, you laughsters!

                                        (Kern, 62)

   While Khlebnikov's poem elaborates on a neologistic play on the Russian word *shmekhat'*, "to laugh," Vladimir Mayakovsky's "Morning" makes use of another form of word play:

Ugryumyi dozhd skosil glaza.	The morose rain looked askance.
A za	Beyond
reshotkoi	The sharp
chotkoi	Grillwork
zheleznoi mysli provodov—	Of the wires' iron thought—
perina.	A featherbed.

I na	And on
neyo	It
vstayushchikh zvyozd	Lightly rest
legko opyorlis nogi.	The feet of awakening stars.
No gi-	But the per-
bel. . . .	dition. . . .

(Brown, 75)

The focus here is on homophonic syllables, which Mayakovsky isolates and repeats in order to increase their ambiguity and to foreground their materiality. There remains nevertheless a clear thematic reference to the Russian Revolution, which like the morning will bring a new day from out of the present darkness. Khlebnikov and Kruchonykh reduced their poetic focus even further, however, to a poetry of neologistic syllables called *zaum,* or transrational poetry. The following poem by Kruchonykh is probably the most famous of the Futurist *zaum* poems, made up entirely of nonsense (or, as Kruchonykh preferred, *trans*sense) syllables:

```
dyr     bul     shchyl
     ubeshchur
        skum
vy     so     bu
r      l      ez
```

(Brown, 58)

The intention, apparent in the term "transrational," is not to do away with meaning but to isolate the building block, so to speak, of meaning—the syllable. Such a practice appears again in the work of Language poet David Melnick. From his work *PCOET* (1972):

```
seta
colecc
puilse, i
canoe
it spear heieo
as Rea, cinct pp
pools we sly drosp
Geianto

     (o sordea, o weedsea!)
```

(*In the American Tree,* 91)

In "A Short Word on My Work" Melnick writes, "What can such poems do for you? You are a spider strangling in your own web, suffocated by meaning. You ask to be freed by these poems from the intolerable burden of trying to understand" (p. 13). Rather than continuing the *zaum* search for the basic units of meaning, Melnick here seems to deny meaning completely. But he goes on to qualify that impression: although the "world of meaning . . . doesn't fit," he nonetheless continues to seek ways of coming to terms with it. To that extent he carries on the *zaum* tradition.

Similar to and roughly contemporaneous with the Futurists, the Dadaists also anticipate some of the formal developments of and to a certain degree the social stance towards the institution of art of Language poetry. The Dada movement strove to reveal the stagnant and corrupt nature of art as an institution of bourgeois society. In "An Introducton to Dada" Tristan Tzara explains that the Dadaists descended from two revolutionary French traditions, the political (the Commune, the Revolution) and the poetic (the literary tradition of Baudelaire, Nerval, Rimbaud, Lautreamont, Mallarmé, Verlaine, Jarry, St. Pol Roux, and Apollinaire). But in the midst of World War I, Tzara and others became disgusted with the social impotence of Aestheticism; they wanted to make poetry and life one. "It seemed to us," Tzara writes, "that the world was losing itself in idle babbling, that literature and art had become institutions located on the margin of life, that instead of serving man they had become the instruments of an outmoded society" up to its knees in war dead (p. 403).

A Dada poem, then, may superficially resemble a poem by Mallarmé or Lautreamont in its attention to language as language rather than as a transparent medium of representation. But the impulse behind Dada was not to extract itself from a rationalistic, mercenary, and intellectually stifling bourgeois society. The Dadaists sought a revolutionary change in society and a reintegration of poetry into daily praxis. The formal techniques of Dadaist poetry were all part of this challenge carried out by rejecting the hegemonic notions of art, by creating an anti-art (see Hans Richter, *Dada: Art and Anti-Art*). In 1916 Hugo Ball gave a reading of his abstract poems, which resemble the Futurists' *zaum* in their foregrounding of sound and rhythm and their use of nonsense words. One of Ball's poems begins: "zimzim urallala zimzim urullala zimzim zanzibar zimzalla zam" (Richter, 43). Unlike Khlebnikov's search for the kernels of meaning, however, Ball's poems were presented as a challenge to the notion that poetry should have meaning at all.

Duchamp's Dada ready-mades challenged a number of institutional aesthetic concepts all at once. The most famous example is his *Fountain* (1917), the urinal which he signed "R. Mutt" and submitted to the first New York Society of Independent Artists exhibition. By submitting an ordinary object to an art show, Duchamp questioned the status of the work of art as something inherently aesthetic; the art status of any object, he implied, depends on a set of unexamined social conventions, not on any quality inherent in the object. Also, by choosing a mass-produced object such as a urinal, he challenged the notion of a single original work as well as the valorization of the individual artist's creative expression, a critique furthered by the signature on the urinal.

Another formal characteristic of some Dada poetry is the use of disjunct syntax, sometimes achieved through chance procedures of composition. Tzara wrote a recipe for making a Dadaist poem: take an article from a newspaper, cut out as many words as you want for the poem, put them in a bag and shake it, then take them out one at a time, writing down each word in the order of its appearance. Tzara's "Manifesto of mr. aa the anti-philosopher" illustrates his manipulations of syntax and his use of discordant series of images:

> I've forgotten something:
> where? why? how?
> in other words:
> ventilator of cold examples will have to serve as a cavalcade to the fragile snake and i never had the pleasure of seeing you my dear rigid the ear will emerge of its own accord from the envelope like all marine confections and the products of the firm of Aa & Co. chewing gum for instance and dogs have blue eyes, I drink camomile tea, they drink wind, Dada introduces new points of view, nowadays people sit at the corners of tables, in attitudes sliding a little to the left and right, that's why I'm angry with Dada, wherever you go insist on the abolition of D's, eat Aa, rub yourself down with Aa toothpaste, buy your clothes from Aa. Aa is a handkerchief and a sex organ wiping its nose, a rapid noiseless—rubber-tired—collapse, needs no manifestoes, or address books, gives a 25% discount buy your clothes from Aa he has blue eyes. (p. 85)

Bruce Andrews's recent work, *I Don't Have Any Paper So Shut Up (Or, Social Romanticism)*, invokes the anger and disgust of Dada, as seen in this excerpt from "Isolate Your Fuse" (1986):

> Isolate your fuse
> my sentimentalization of hatred juggling for Jesus; hardware sweats at bedside discipline can be good detective, time for the blanket show. I wish into chocolate that's bloodhound prone facts, make prime less waste—if only I had strangled it in its tank.
> I'm too proud to think
> you want to be liberated but basically you're just a dental supply fixture, shoot them in the head to anesthetize them; hype anchors the argument like Mary Poppins under the thumb of a filthy vein body just another android fun machine. Quadriculus circuli sweethearts maneuver their sanitary napkins into impenetrable cabinetry; startled starlets squared by squids, alla-y'all sucker sucker muhfuhs—punk beliefs can be bought. 6 trolls out of 7 news be sweat holiday prophylactic fishhead bloodclot—meanwhile back at the political.
> Who wears the blonde wig in *that* family? Dollies hurt leg: I feel whoops shame;
>   A perfectly glandular reprisal, hog-heaven for the fashion-tyrannized I recommend a transplant—rock of the weenies
> those bottles will seek their own salvation. Vietnam tastes better: do ten seconds of fake mambo, spawn a tress shit
> sticky history of perfection. What positions
> your rights at the bidet flowering penis choreography, it's supposed to get harder if you're being strangled; why don't you just pest off?

Unleased disposition schemers, this is soup to be defoliated, just the right corporate body as eating roast tractor parts. I'd sell my government, to these men, any day. look for quick profits in communist misfortune. I AM SOMEBODY It's a Fun World friends you to buy their own money Because Politics Stinks, act insecure & put other people at ease. I went from Hegel to Mighty Atom comix
Afro-cubist that mass equals crass dim men pop
a sauce that monsters fault.

The disjunct syntax, semantic shifts, and reflexive language of Tzara's work also anticipate the techniques used by some of the Language poets. From Kit Robinson's "Authority Vespers":

May try industrious lapping at lakeside. Old habit at a glance, but punctilious rails glean rye. All I've ever envisaged careens floorboardward in an imagination of tiles. Try to pry information off fuselage, push raw metal endeavor tied to a post. Tangled organ's were Gorky's parking spot. There's air outside an idea, more space than meets the eye. The pull is furious, flag snap in storm. All along the warm interior of the mouth houses resource. The elevated crash diction completes the image sentence. But behind that these interpolations can never get, the base slides noiselessly under foot, buildings heave into view, and an accelerated procedure takes up the slacks and drapes them over a chair.

The dream-like quality of Robinson's "Authority Vespers" also recalls the work of the French Surrealists. The distinction, formally speaking, between a Dada and a Surreal poem is, of course, a dubious one, especially considering that many of the Dadaists went on to become Surrealists. The distinction is one of emphasis: whereas Tzara insisted that "If there is a system in the lack of system—that of my proportions—I never apply it" ("Manifesto of mr. aa," 85), André Breton, the leader of Surrealism, insisted on systematizing the techniques and assumptions of Dada, shifting the school's emphasis from nihilism to surrealism. Breton justifies the shift as follows:

Postwar disorder, a state of mind essentially anarchic that guided that cycle's many manifestations, a deliberate refusal to judge—for lack, it was said, of criteria—the actual qualifications of the individuals, and, perhaps, in the last analysis, a certain spirit of negation which was making itself conspicuous, had brought about a dissolution of the group (which one might say, from its dispersed and heterogeneous character, was inchoate), whose germinating force has nevertheless been decisive and, by general consent of present-day critics, has greatly influenced the course of ideas. (*What is Surrealism?*, 119–20)

Quite appropriately, the particular direction poetry should then take came to Breton as he was drifting off to sleep one night and a sentence formed in his mind with no clear "trace of any relation whatever to any incidents I may at that time have been involved in . . .: 'A man is cut in half by the window' " (p. 120). Thus the dream, and behind it the Freudian unconscious, became the focal point of Surrealism. The poetic challenge to logic was carried out no longer in the name of meaninglessness but now in the name of supreme meaning, *sur*-realism. "We still live under the reign of logic," Breton claimed. "But the methods of logic are applied nowadays only to the resolution of problems of secondary interest. . . . It is only by what seems pure chance that there has recently been brought to light an aspect of mental life—to my belief by far the most important—with which it was supposed we no longer had any concern. Credit for these discoveries must go to Freud" (p. 124).

The poet of the Language school to follow this lead most closely is Nick Piombino, a practicing psychoanalyst. In "Writing and Free Association" (*L=A=N=G=U=A=G=E* 1, 1 [February 1978]), he identifies "automatic writing" with an attempt "to read, write, and understand poetry that directs attention to the *totality* of the thinking process." Poetry, then, provides an approach to the state of mind in which, according to Breton, "life and death, the real and the imaginary, the high and the low, are not perceived as contradictions" (*What Is Surrealism?*, 129). Piombino continues:

> Like the sequential motifs in dreams, a poem's meaning often appears to be more verbal than literal, resonating with meaning rather than describing it. Sometimes sequences in poems (and dreams and thoughts) can be drawn together like fragments in a collage, to open another implied area not yet found. What is before can become what is next (to). For example, in writing poetry the very next thought may seem technically unacceptable but allowed to remain in the poem may reveal an otherwise hidden intention.

Piombino's statements above aptly describe the Surrealist focus on the sequence of motifs, the drift from image to image which "may reveal an otherwise hidden intention" or unity. But Piombino's emphasis, as he later explains in "Writing and Experiencing," is on the "relationship of this (the problem of the human relationship to space, matter, and time) to the appeal of *density*, or rapid experiences of strong emotional impact directly juxtaposed against the material facticity of language" (*LB*, 71). The image as Breton saw it transcends the medium of presentation, language, and in fact passes wholly through translation from one language to another. Language does not escape so easily from view, however, for Piombino. Writing, "like a forgotten ruin or monument, . . . continues to haunt us in its facticity as object" and enters into "paradoxical relationships to memory (invested in the image)" (*LB*, 72). The mutability of the image due to the endless possibilities of linguistic man-ifestations makes language "the enemy of the state and historicity because of its power to germinate systems antithetical to custom because custom is partly dependent on coded laws." The ambiguity of signification foregrounded in poetry thus challenges the hegemonic paradigms of experience.

The role of the "material facticity of language" distinguishes Piombino's poetry from Breton's. A look at the process and function of image shifts in both a Breton poem and a Piombino one should illustrate this difference. Breton:

At the hour of love and blue eyelids
I see myself burning in turn I see that solemn hidingplace of
    nothings
That was my body
Probed by the patient beak of the fire-ibis
When it is finished I enter into the invisible ark
Paying no attention to the passers-by of life whose dragging
    footsteps echo in the distance
I see the ridges of the sun

(Selected Poems, 63)

Piombino:

Modelled after an aolde method of practice
Memory, spliced from itself, the smile
The possibilities. The list, the account,
Positive attitude, now rise: what if
The furniture, the couch is $800, and
Don't ask, slips past the diamonds, this
Copied from an old format, brush stroked,
The wood veneer, the bicycle, marginal stories,
The opening is a disclosure, the spreading fan
And, pumping hard, an explosion, the best is possible,
So that four degrees, the earth tilting,
A visual gyre, that is, circling around the cameraman
Spots crevices in the apparent surface,
A recording of mute repetitions lying beneath
X speech. Cancel, amour, follows closely.
And writ large: CAMEL, obscure ("that's right!")
Applied, approved, method of practice:
No repetitions please, penitent, that you have to follow
Time to continue. . . .

(Poems, 14)

Certainly there is a fluidity of imagery in Piombino's poem. But the shifts
are due to a protean language which breaks down, changing syntactical and
grammatical patterns before the sentence can state anything clearly. The
reader's attention is drawn immediately to the linguistic level of the poem by
the unusual use of "aolde" and the reflexive statement in the first line which
foregrounds the poem at the level of "method of practice." "Modelled"
demands a referent from the independent clause which should (but doesn't)
follow, but is "Memory" that referent? The next modifying phrase, "spliced
from itself," also hangs without a referent: From itself to what? Nevertheless,
though grammatically incomplete, the phrase and the entire "sentence" unit
do make sense within the film metaphor, seen as various phrases spliced
together in jump cuts, parataxis undercutting the hypotaxis implied by the
phrases. What follows, however, is no simple collage. Instead of a series of

images, Piombino presents a series of conflicting grammatical units and reflexive statements: "Applied, approved, method of practice:/ No repetitions please. . . ."

Barrett Watten sees his own practice as an extension of Surrealism, but he is drawn more to the social role that Breton carved out for himself than to any specific set of aesthetic or psychological assumptions. For instance, Watten rejects any notion of an unconscious or the inherent value of free association (see "Watten Interview"), but he endorses Breton's attempt to create a life in which poetry and politics are one.

The "Manifesto for an Independent Revolutionary Art" (1938), written by Breton and Leon Trotsky, proclaims:

> True art, which is not content to play variations on ready-made models but rather insists on expressing the inner needs of man and of mankind in its time—true art is unable not to be revolutionary, not to aspire to a complete and radical reconstruction of society. (*What Is Surrealism?*, 184)

At a time when Soviet Communism and European Fascism were stamping out intellectual dissent, any art that fostered intellectual development, Breton and Trotsky claimed, necessarily furthered the mental and consequently the political liberation of humanity. For Breton, as Watten points out, the self or "single artist, is becoming the locus of a collective voice" (*Total Syntax*, 39). The single artist's identification with "exterior fact" (for Breton, the revolutionary movements of the 1930s) through his or her adoption of a consciously revolutionary role becomes the paradigm of artistic posture or "method" for Watten: "The test of a 'politics of poetry' is in the entry of poetry into the world in a political way" (*L=A=N=G=U=A=G=E* 4 [Winter 1982]: 129).

Recognizing that the social conditions which offered Breton the opportunity for such an identification have long been gone, Watten sees the need for today's poet to approach the self in poetry reflexively, the self no longer in the position to be the "locus of a collective voice." What does this look like in practice? Watten attempts to clarify this in his discussion of Kit Robinson's poem, "In the American Tree":

> . . . although the landscape is mutating, the driver is always in control of the car. The attention is directed to the progression in the poem, and the image content is undercut and distanced by that fact. Illusion comes with a tag. The transformation in Robinson's poem is not the coming into being of the image but of something even deeper—the perception of mind in control of its language. Distance, rather than absorption, is the intended effect. (*Total Syntax*, 64)

Despite the disjunct and random appearance of much Language poetry, control remains central for Watten.

Control in the midst of chaos was also central for the Objectivist poet Louis Zukofsky, another significant model for the Language school. In "Notes for

Echo Lake 3" Michael Palmer eulogizes Zukofsky's death. Palmer's poem is a meditation on the aesthetics of Zukofsky:

> The letters of the words of our legs and arms. What he had seen or thought he'd seen within the eye, voices overheard rising and falling. And if each conversation has no end, then composition is a placing beside or with and is endless, broken threads of cloud driven from the west by afternoon wind. (*Notes for Echo Lake*, 16)

The reference is predominantly to Zukofsky's 1930 essay, "An Objective," in which he outlined the requirements for Objectivist poetry. The essay opens with the optical definition of an Objective: "The lens bringing the rays from an object to a focus" (Prepositions, 20). Zukofsky wanted a writing "which is the detail, not the mirage, of seeing, of thinking with the things as they exist, and of directing them along a line of melody" (p. 20). Poets should not waste their time on the imprecision of metaphor and useless words used only to complete a metric pattern; nor should they subordinate poetry to something else (such as philosophy or politics). Poets instead should focus on an array of individual objects and should structure those objects into a "rested totality"— the poem itself seen as an object thoroughly organized like a musical composition. Here we see once again a poet emphasizing the material object-status of the word and downplaying its referential role—Palmer's "The letters of the words of . . ."—although Zukofsky insists that the sign be used "outside as well as within the context [of the poem] with communicative reference" (p. 24). Zukofsky chose his *A-7* to represent his Objectivist work in the *Objectivist Anthology* he edited in 1930:

> Horses: who will do it? out of manes? Words
> Will do it, out of manes, out of airs, but
> They have no manes, so there are no airs, birds
> Of words, from me to them no singing gut.
> For they have no eyes, for their legs are wood,
> For their stomachs are logs with print on them;
> Blood red, red lamps hang from necks or where could
> Be necks, two legs stand A, four together M.
> "Street Closed" is what print says on their stomachs;
> That cuts out everybody but the diggers;
> You're cut out, and she's cut out, and the jiggers
> Are cut out. No! we can't have such nor bucks
>   As won't, tho they're not here, pass thru a hoop
>   Strayed on a manhole—me? Am on a stoop.
>
>   (p. 39)

As critic Hugh Kenner points out, *A-7* is made up of seven sonnets, each with an ababcdcd octave, this one with a sestet of effegg. "The diction, the rhythms, the objects handled, are comically inappropriate to these Renaissance formalisms, and the dexterity with which forms mutate make the clumsy words and objects tumble as though weightless through an intricate juggling act . . . precisely as in music, where there isn't a burden of 'meaning' and playing can seem like play" ("Two Pieces on 'A'," 190). I would argue, however, that playing isn't only play in this movement: a tension mounts even within the first sonnet between the words that play and the words that say. "Street Closed" is not only a physical object pasted to the wooden belly of a sawhorse but also a sign of exclusion. Those who work are protected from those who do not. The jiggers are "cut out" from the work area, left idle on the stoop during the height of the Great Depression. Zukofsky's isolation of the material word is not simply an aesthetician's game; it is an exploration of the power of words and the structures that order those words. The ideal order, as we have seen, is music. But here there is "from me to them no singing gut."

What distinguishes Zukofsky's exploration of the word from that of many Language poets is the locus of attention of each. Zukofsky focuses on the shaping power of perception, the human ability to string a series of objects together into a meaningful whole. But his interest in perception is not epistemological—"I don't care how you think about things, whether you think they are outside you, even if you disappear, or if they exist only because you think of them" ("Sincerity and Objectification," 266). Zukofsky is concerned with the practical necessity of shaping the flux outside us; while scientists grapple with the "problem of infinity," the good poet "integrates any human emotion, any discourse, into an order of words that exists as another created thing in the world, to affect it and be judged by it" (*Prepositions*, 28).

The locus of attention of many Language poets, however, is extended out beyond the horizon of the mind's act of ordering to the ordering of that mind itself. The focus is now on the ideological framing of perception. Zukofsky seemed to take for granted that anyone could learn to focus his or her attention on an object and then see it clearly, see it just as anyone else would see it. All that was needed was a disciplined mind. But "All meaning is a construct," Silliman writes, "built from the determinate code of language" ("If by 'Writing'," 168), those language codes in turn determined within a particular social formation. Foregrounding the signifier's materiality for Silliman grows not out of a desire to impose order on flux but to show all such orderly impositions as historically relative. We "are initiated by language into a (the) world," explains Charles Bernstein, "and we see and understand the world through the terms and meanings that come into play in this acculturation, a coming into culture where culture is the form of community, of a collectivity" (*LB*, 60). Even Watten, who in his call for order and organization through the self's "identification with its objects" (*Total Syntax*, 59) seems quite Zukofskian, expands that horizon by insisting also that the "objects and contexts of art are relative and continuous" (p. 66).

So far I have been discussing relatively distant precursors whose works in one way or another resemble that of many of the Language poets, and whose names come up quite often in the critical writings and discussions of the latter. But the most immediate and influential poetic context out of which Language poetry has developed is what since 1960 has been called "The New American Poetry." It was in that year Donald Allen published *The New American Poetry* anthology, which presented to a wide audience the work of poets such as Charles Olson, Robert Duncan, Robert Creeley (from the so-called Black Mountain school) and John Ashbery, Kenneth Koch, and Frank O'Hara from the New York School, as well as Allen Ginsberg, Gary Snyder, and many others. The one common characteristic of the forty-four poets represented in the anthology, Allen explains in the preface, is their "total rejection of all those qualities typical of academic verse" (qualities I will soon discuss). "They are our true avant-garde," Allen continues, "the true containers of the modern movement in American poetry."

The poet who set the tone for the poetry and poetics of the New American poetry was Charles Olson. It is in his essay "Projective Verse" (1950) that the lines are drawn between those working out of the tradition of Pound and Williams and those perpetuating the "claustrophobic" tradition of academic verse. Academic verse—"The Non-Projective," the "verse which print bred"—is "closed" verse, characterized by a concentration on the poet's ego, and a reliance on the metrical line, the stanza, logical argument, description, hypotactic syntax, and conventional grammar. Such writing does not engage the objects of the world; it only examines them.

In contrast, projective verse, or "what can also be called COMPOSITION BY FIELD," is open verse. The poem should be seen not as a series of lines tacked to the left margin but as an open field into which the poet ventures, putting "himself in the open—he can go by no track other than the one the poem under hand declares, for itself" ("Projective Verse," 148). As we can see here, Olson is resurrecting the organicism of the Romantic poets as a weapon against the new classicism of non-projective verse. Following Ernest Fenellosa and Ezra Pound, Olson sees the poem as "a high energy-construct and, at all points, an energy discharge" from the poet to the reader. Here is one sense of the term "projective": the projection of energy, which Olson identifies as "the kinetics of the thing" (p. 148). Traditional meter and rhyme patterns will drain energy rather than discharge it.

But Olson recognizes that simply putting himself in the open will not guarantee that energy-transfer. There is still at least one principle to be followed if random chaos or flat, drab poems are to be avoided: "FORM IS NEVER MORE THAN AN EXTENSION OF CONTENT." But what does this mean in practice? Olson's third point is "the *process* of the thing, how the principle can be made so to shape the energies that the form is accomplished. I think it can be boiled down to one statement . . .: ONE PERCEPTION MUST IMMEDIATELY AND DIRECTLY LEAD TO A FURTHER PERCEPTION" (pp. 148–49). Now the poem is projective in the sense that there is a constant shifting of images, voices, and contexts. From Olson's "The Kingfishers":

I thought of the E on the stone, and of what Mao said
la lumiere"
             but the kingfisher
de l'aurore"
             but the kingfisher flew west
est devant nous!"
                   he got the color of his breast
                   from the heat of the setting sun!

The features are, the feebleness of the feet (syndactylism of the 3rd & 4th digit)
the bill, serrated, sometimes a pronounced beak, the wings
where the color is, short and round, the tail
inconspicuous.

But not these things are the factors. Not the birds.
The legends are
legends. Dead, hung up indoors, the kingfisher
will not indicate a favoring wind,
or avert the thunderbolt. Nor, by its nesting,
still the waters, with the new year,
for seven days.
It is true, it does nest with the opening year,
but not on the waters.
It nests at the end of a tunnel bored by itself in a bank. There,
six or eight white and translucent eggs are laid, on fishbones
not on bare clay, on bones thrown up in pellets by the birds.

                                        On these rejectamenta
(as they accumulate they form a cup-shaped structure) the young are born.
And, as they are fed and grow, this nest of excrement and decayed fish becomes
                                                    a dripping, fetid mass

Mao concluded:
              nous devons
                       nous lever
                             et agir!
                                                        (pp. 2–3)

For Olson such open form on the page was not intended solely as a visual
shift from the left margin but also as a score for performance. Each line is a
measure of breath rather than a certain number of metric feet; each space is a
measured rest scored so as to return poetry to "its producer and reproducer,
the voice, . . . its place of origin *and* its destination" (p. 153). It is through
speech that the person, in combining breath and ear, takes his or her place
among the objects of the world. If the poet "chooses to speak from these roots
[breath, sound, language, then he] works in that area where nature has given
him size, projective size" (p. 156).

Perhaps more than anyone else, Silliman has made the most coherent attempt to place Language poetry in a line extending from the Projectivist poets. Such an extension, however, is not always clear even in Silliman's writings. As we shall see, while he does make clear where Language writing departs from the pronouncements in "Projective Verse," Silliman's claims for extending the Black Mountain tradition in the name of its "higher principles" are never really explained. He does write that much contemporary poetry—not simply Language poetry—grows out of Projectivism, and one must assume that by this Silliman means in part that Olson, Duncan, and Creeley set the tone for how non-academic poetry would be discussed in the following decades. Any poet in recent years, then, will most likely have chosen either to work in or against the Black Mountain frame. More specifically, however, one can see Language writing as continuing the emphasis on "open" verse, what Duncan has called opening the field. If projective verse was dedicated to expanding the possibilities for poetry in a time when the lyric form, examined by New Critical standards, seemed to many to have exhausted itself—Robert Lowell's "Skunk Hour" supposedly revealing the decadence inherent from the start in the emphasis on the self—then Language poetry continues that opening of the possibilities of verse at a point when Projectivist assumptions themselves in turn appear to have reached a dead end.

One can see another general influence, furthermore, in Black Mountain's establishment of a close-knit poetic community in which poets worked together in developing the possibilities of a poetic tradition without the support of the academic world. While the Black Mountain community itself has virtually disappeared, the Language communities of San Francisco, Washington, D.C., and New York City have created an extensive communications network for sharing their work and ideas.

The Language school's departure from Black Mountain, as I have suggested, is much more obvious in the critical writings of the former. Silliman claims that Robert Grenier and Barrett Watten, in their editing of *This* magazine beginning in 1971, provided the possibility (the necessity) of an articulation of the limits of Black Mountain poetics. It "was the particular contribution of *This*, in rejecting a speech-based poetics and consciously raising the issue of reference, to suggest that any new direction would require poets to look (in some ways for the first time) at what a poem is actually made of—not images, not voice, not characters or plot, all of which appear on paper, or in one's mouth, only through the invocation of a specific medium, language itself" (*In the American Tree*, xvi).

In the work of Clark Coolidge, Silliman explains elsewhere, such writing in language "meant freeing words from whatever context forced them to be less than themselves" ("Ubeity," 19), a claim reminiscent of Khlebnikov's call for "the word as such." Like Zukofsky's, Coolidge's work approaches the condition of music. But Coolidge's music is Bop, not Bach. "In Bop," Coolidge writes, "especially in its drums which almost purely color and are colored by time itself, there is the sense that sheer continuance gets articulated" ("A Note on Bop"). Coolidge's is the music of process, not of control. From *The Maintains:*

> for the fade use of smart mined mode
> firmly in fast by act do another
> plaster link phrase to protozoa
> hawser of tie adipose
> wealth spun ant lean
> tire vessel top score
> flag hind such as vole
> interval side in such field more
> gottlieb blenny
>
> (*The Maintains,* 70)

In addition to Coolidge's attention to rhythm, we can see here again the emphasis on the material quality of the word which he shares with Zukofsky. But not all Language poets share this particular way of focusing on the medium itself. In "Notes on Coolidge, Objectives, Zukofsky, Romanticism, and &" Robert Grenier responds to Zukofsky's and Coolidge's efforts to make works into objects: "Ouch. Paint is paint. What a circle" (p. 17). Although Grenier himself explores the material side of words—especially sound—his purpose is not to separate the word from meaning but to examine how the particular material word (versus its supposed synonym) influences and enhances meaning:

> Again, question of *how* words further perception, act in same place same time as mind's experience of objects in situation, like a third party (a sentence) tells & shows you what's happening. Language as operationally interactive definition, or some such, but that's my need. (pp. 18–19)

Awareness of such a concern helps one to explain Grenier's fascination with minimal semantic units, resonating with meaning potential, as in the following poem from *A Day at the Beach* (1984):

VOICE SAYS
v o i c e s

Such a poem depends on the printed page, for we most likely would fail to distinguish between these homophones when spoken. Ironically, then, the ambiguity of the heard meaning colors what is said, the voice being not capable of speaking clearly about itself. Furthermore, we could not distinguish between the uppercase line and the underlined lowercase one, both exhibiting graphemic devices implying a vocal stress—stress itself being meaningless in the absence of other non-stressed terms. One would be hard put to devise a more thorough challenge to the Projectivist valorization of speech.

Grenier also insists on the influence that his Selectric typewriter has on the meaning of the poem, giving each letter equal space versus the n-space, m-space, and so on of the printing press. "Type is like a window," Grenier claims. "The shape of the world is contributed to by the language forms we have made. . . . The results gained come from a reformulation of letter values. Rearranging letters is alchemy" ("Typewriter vs. Typeface," 7). Olson's composition by field is put to use with a vengeance, no longer as a score for voice but as a visual artifact whose "meaning," like that of any visual art, exists on the page itself. The page *is* the field. (I should concede here that the same is true for some of Olson's later work. See especially *The Maximus Poems: Volume Three,* pp. 104 and 121.)

Another major New American influence on certain Language poets is the New York School, especially John Ashbery. The most influential Ashbery text is *The Tennis Court Oath* (1962), which critic Harold Bloom has called "the outrageously disjunctive volume," flawed because Ashbery "attempted too massive a swerve away from the ruminative continuities of Stevens and Whitman" ("John Ashbery," 111). But it is precisely the book's swerve from rumination and continuity that makes it such an important model for contemporary poets. These qualities are evident in the poem "White Roses":

The worst side of it all—
The white sunlight on the polished floor—
Pressed into service,
And then the window closed
And the night ends and begins again.
Her face goes green, her eyes are green,
In the dark corner playing "The Stars and Stripes Forever." I try to
    describe for you,
But you will not listen, you are like the swan.

Of the Language poets, Andrews has written perhaps the most extensive critical response to *The Tennis Court Oath.* In "Misrepresentation" (*L=A=N=G=U=A=G=E* 12 [1980]) Andrews claims that Ashbery's book "poses for us a radical questioning of established forms, yet at the same time, and so appropriately in its own form, it explores the implications of that questioning—not as an idea, but as an experience and a *reading.*" The work demands, in other words, "Behavioral reading, rather than hermeneutic ones." Through his "convulsed" syntax, his "jagged kaleidoscope" of images, and his interruptions of tone, Ashbery questions language's ability to represent as well as our desire to represent, our need to expose the world and ourselves in the light of day. "I try to/ describe for you," Ashbery writes, but he recognizes that "no stars are there/ No stripes,/ But a blind man's cane poking. . . ." Once one has recognized the inherent opacity of the word, the social contract behind its supposed transparency, "it makes sense to be skeptical, to embody in *composition* the doubt that transparency is more than a devious & second-best fraud, fraught with an illusory naturalism, a making into nature what is really our *production*." The answer is not, however, to give up on language and meaning—why write if such were the case?—but to put forward a writing of self-conscious production that recognizes the arbitrary but necessary choices behind what we determine as "truth."

Charles Bernstein is one contemporary poet to benefit from Ashbery's "swerve" from Stevens and Whitman (if it is a swerve—one could possibly argue for a disruption of ruminative continuity even in parts of their work.) Andrews's discussion of *The Tennis Court Oath*, for instance, applies equally well to many poems in Bernstein's *Controlling Interests* (1980). From "Matters of Policy":

> On a broad plain in a universe of
> anterooms, making signals in the dark, you
> fall down on your waistband &, carrying your
> own plate, a last serving, set out for
> another glimpse of a gaze. In a room
> full of kids splintering like gas jets against
> shadows of tropical taxis—he really had, I
> should be sorry, I think this is the ("I
> know I have complained" "I am quite well"
> "quit nudging")—croissants
> outshine absinthe as "la plus, plus sans
> egal" though what *I* most care about
> is another sip of my Pepsi-Cola. Miners
> tell me about the day, like a pack of
> cards, her girlfriend split for Toronto. . . .
>
> (p. 1)

The disjunct syntax, the incomplete statements, and the radical shifts of imagery all recall Ashbery's early work. But what does not occur in "Matters of Policy" is the tortured meditation on perception and representation. Such questioning has been digested during the fifteen or so years intervening between "White Roses" and Bernstein's poem. The essential insight of Ashbery's work—the social production of meaning—now becomes the dominant focus, enlisted in an examination of the politics of the use of language. Irony is posed in Bernstein's work not just as a questioning of language but as a guard against ideological contamination.

In "Misrepresentation" Andrews sees Ashbery's work as the germ for "an Ideologiecritik, and a critique of clarity and transparency and language . . . ; and hierarchy arising historically at the same time as instrumental literacy (Levi-Strauss) or the incest taboo." The notion of poetry as ideology critique, as a specific mode of ideological struggle, associates much Language poetry with the various avant-garde manifestations which occurred earlier in this century. It is to that question that I turn in the next chapter.

T W O

Ideological Struggle and the Possibility of an Oppositional Poetic Practice

One of the crucial issues in discussions of Louis Althusser's conception of ideology is the problem of functionalism. At the heart of this issue is the question of agency, in particular the possibility of an opposition within and the revolutionary transformation of a given mode of production. The story is that Althusser has conceptualized the relationship between ideology and the reproduction of the relations of production in such a way that the possibility of opposition or revolution is denied; once a mode of production is established and begins interpellating subjects through its Ideological State Apparatuses, there is no release valve in Althusser's conceptual machine that provides for the death of a mode of production. There is no way to account for the arrival in society of oppositional forces which seek to criticize the status quo and to think their way through to more egalitarian relations of production—oppositional forces such as some of the so-called Language poets.

Or so the story goes. We are speaking, of course, of a reading of Althusser's celebrated text "Ideology and Ideological State Apparatuses" *(Lenin and Philosophy,* 127–86; hereafter cited as *Lenin).* We are speaking, furthermore, of the very question of reading itself in regards to the writer of *Reading Capital* (Althusser), for whom "ideology" is a process of writing the world so as to provide certain readings of that world, and for whom "science"—or rather "scientific practice"—is a reading of that reading/writing/constitution of the "real." When Althusser talks about ideology as a "representation" of the imaginary relationship of individuals to their real conditions of existence *(Lenin,* 162), he presents us with a process of textualization. In this light a given social formation is thus the site of inscription; the subject is a text. Which brings me to three separate but related points:

1. Those who argue that Althusser's conception of the reproduction of the relations of production depends on a functionalist view of the role of ideology thus argue that Althusser presents us with a closed text, written once and for all. But I will argue that Althusser's notion of social formation, even in his essay on Ideological State Apparatuses (ISA), provides us with an antidote to such a functionalist reading of ideology.

2. The notion of ideology as textualization offers a bridge between Marxist ideology critique and Derrida's notion of dissemination, as Thomas E. Lewis has pointed out in "Reference and Dissemination: Althusser After Derrida." If discussions of ideology are also discussions of representation, then Marxism cannot afford to ignore the developments in contemporary theories of reading/writing for, as Fredric Jameson claims, the "kind of decipherment of which literary and textual criticism is in many ways the strong form" serves as the model for the very analytic practice put forward by Althusser *(The Political Unconscious,* 296).

3. I argue furthermore that the conception of reading as the constitution of its object—in other words, the writing of that object—points to a conception of literary practice not just as the object of criticism but as a mode of intervention in ideological struggle. When that practice becomes conscious of itself as a practice *as such* (when it becomes a "scientific practice," as Althusser would say), then that literary practice may serve as a mode of ideology critique on a par with theoretical practice. The poetic practice I have in mind is that of some Language poets today.

My thesis is that Althusser's conception of ideology as a writing and framing of our social relations provides not simply a functional analysis of the conceptual limits imposed by particular ideologies—although it does provide that—but also a glimpse of the possibilities for opposition within any ideological formation. In other words, rather than denying the political effectivity of any and all oppositional practices, Althusser's ISA essay shows how practices such as Language poetry can come about despite the power of the hegemonic modes of ideological interpellation.

I begin with a reading of the ISA essay. It is extremely hard, Althusser claims, "to raise oneself to the *point of view of reproduction.* Nevertheless, everything outside this point of view remains abstract (worse than one-sided: distorted)—even at the level of production, and, *a fortiori,* at that of mere practice" *(Lenin,* 128; his emphasis). *Mere practice* at the level of production: such is the focus of empiricist studies. What such a focus leaves out of view is the "endless chain" (p. 129) of the relations between production, consumption, and the realization of surplus value which are necessary for the reproduction of the forces of production (the *forces* and the *relations* of production making up the conditions of production). The production process, consequently, cannot be viewed as autotelic (existing solely at the level of the company) but as a "global," endless metonymic chain of relations within the social formation. I insist on repeating the term "social formation" here because such a conception continually qualifies any attempt to focus solely on the concept of "mode of production." The social formation in Althusser's work is not seen as the *expression* of the dominant mode of production but as the greater or lesser structural qualification of that dominant mode. At the risk of offending my readers, I wish to point out—as if it were not already pointed out in the many readings of Althusser—that Althusser's conception of structure in dominance is not that of a closed system, an impenetrable fortress with no egress, but that of a complex and conflictual articulation of competing modes of production. Althusser's own conception of structural causality does not allow for the purely functionalist notion of ideology attributed to him. But this remains to be seen.

Althusser discusses this conception of structural causality, of course, in *Reading Capital:*

> The structure is not an essence *outside* the economic phenomena which comes and alters their aspect, forms and relations and which is effective on them as an absent cause, *absent because outside them. The absence of the cause in the structure's "metonymic causality" on its effects is not the fault of the exteriority of the structure with respect to the economic phenomena; on the contrary, it is the very form of the structure, as a structure, in its effects.* This implies therefore that the effects are not outside the structure, are not a pre-existing object, element or space in which the structure arrives *to imprint its mark:* on the contrary, it implies that the structure is immanent in its effects, a cause immanent in its effects in the Spinozist sense of the term, that *the whole existence of the structure consists of its effects,* in short that the structure, which is merely a specific combination of its peculiar elements, is nothing outside its effects. (p. 188–89; italics in original)

The nature of that specific combination of the structure's peculiar elements is metonymy. In a note we read that "metonymic causality" is an "expression Jacques-Alain Miller has introduced to characterize a form of structural causality registered in Freud by Jacques Lacan" (p. 188), referring to Freud's notion of the process of displacement of psychic forces in the unconscious. Metonymy, then, is not simply a relationship of contiguity (a static system of elements sitting idly beside one another) but a process of displacement of elements along the relational chain. The notion of metonymic causality is a way of registering the immanence, in other words, of class struggle within the structure itself.

In his ISA essay Althusser argues that:

> the Ideological Apparatuses may be not only the *stake,* but also the *site* of class struggle, and often of bitter forms of class struggle. The class (or class alliance) in power cannot lay down the law in the ISAs as easily as it can in the (repressive) State Apparatuses, not only because the former ruling classes are able to retain strong positions there for a long time, but also because the resistance of the exploited classes is able to find means and occasions to express itself there, either by utilization of their contradictions, or by conquering combat positions in them in struggle. (p. 147; italics in original)

The ISAs themselves—those material loci of ideological interpellation—are not homogeneous spaces of unadulterated indoctrination but instead contradictory articulations of various class (and nonclass) discourses. They are "multiple, distinct, 'relatively autonomous' and capable of providing an objective field to contradictions which express, *in forms which may be limited or extreme,* the effects of the clashes between the capitalist class struggle and the proletarian class struggle, as well as their subordinate forms" (p. 149; italics mine). We can see here that behind the central question of how the reproduction of the relations of production is secured is the very real possibility that it *might not be* secured. Although the ideological field often is like a "concert . . . dominated by a single score" (the ruling ideology), it nevertheless is "occasionally disturbed by contradictions" (the residual influence of former ruling classes as well as the nascent influence of the emergent class) (p. 154).

What this means, I would suggest, is that Althusser's conception of the ISAs, far from denying the possibility of opposition, is inscribed throughout with opposition. If, as Etienne Balibar suggests, Althusser's work "confirms that *the category of practice is the fundamental category* of the materialist dialectic" ("From Bachelard to Althusser," 225; italics in original), then how is it that his work can be read as a theory which denies oppositional practice? One possibility is that some readers have failed to a greater or lesser degree to distinguish between Althusser's discussions of *particular ideologies* and of *ideology in general.* For instance, Thomas Lewis writes:

> Now, if these functions [of the ideological reproduction of the relations of production] are construed as completely determinant of their concepts, and if these concepts are articulated in a relation of correspondence to one another, then the concept of "mode of production" must be seen as designating an *eternal structure.* That is, once it is conceived that productive forces and relations "correspond" and that they functionally reproduce themselves in this relation of correspondence, it becomes impossible to theorize any conditions under which something on the order of a "transitional" phase of "noncorrespondence" can occur. This means, of course, not only that no account can be rendered of past historical change, but also that no strategy can be calculated for promoting future historical change; it also explains why the issue of functionalism is so important for Marxist theory today. ("Reference," 51; italics in original)

Yes, *If* these functions are construed as completely determinant and *if* these concepts are articulated in a relation of correspondence to one another. But as Althusser has insisted time and again, these functions are determinant not completely but in the last instance. And the relation between the forces of production and the relations of production are conceived not as a one-to-one correspondence but as an overdetermined metonymic chain of unevenly developed, relatively autonomous instances. If the ISAs functioned in the way Lewis describes above, then there would be no need whatsoever for the *Repressive* State Apparatuses in Althusser's theory. Why would Althusser bother to discuss "the Government, the Administration, the Army, the Police, the Courts, the Prisons, etc." (*Lenin,* 142–43), if he conceived of a system of automatic reproduction through the ISAs? Furthermore, as Nicos Poulantzas's work attests, the Althusserian conception of "mode of production" is an

abstraction from the interdeterminate articulation of various modes of production existing simultaneously within any given social formation. Althusser's discussion of mode of production and relations of production takes place
within his discussion of ideology in general, a pure and abstract concept that
must be substituted by talk of particular ideologies when we speak of specific
practices.

Let me stretch this point further: even in his discussion of ideology in
general, Althusser provides for the possibility of oppositional practice. All
"*ideology hails or interpellates concrete individuals as concrete subjects,* by the
functioning of the category of the subject" (p. 173; italics in original). These
subjects "are inserted into practices governed by the rituals of the ISAs" (p.
181). The ISAs determine who it is we recognize in "the mutual recognition
of subjects and Subject, the subjects' recognition of each other, and finally the
subject's recognition of himself" (p. 181). Thus:

> caught in this quadruple system of interpellation as subjects, of subjection to the
> Subject, of universal recognition and of absolute guarantee, the subjects "work",
> they "work by themselves" in the vast majority of cases, *with the exception of the
> "bad subjects"* who on occasion provoke the intervention of one of the detachments
> of the (repressive) State apparatus. (p. 181; italics mine)

If individuals are always subjects within certain ideological configurations
even before birth, then what makes these bad subjects possible? In his
post-script Althusser answers this question:

> the ISAs are not the realization of idealogy *in general,* nor even the conflict-free
> realization of the ideology of the ruling class. The ideology of the ruling class does
> not become the ruling ideology by the grace of God, nor even by virtue of the
> seizure of State power alone. It is by the installation of the ISAs in which this
> ideology is realized and realizes itself that it becomes the ruling ideology. But this
> installation is not achieved all by itself; on the contrary, it is the stake in a very
> bitter and continous class struggle: first against the former ruling classes and their
> positions in the old and new ISAs, then against the exploited class. (p. 184–85)

We may now enumerate some reasons why the multiple subjects in a
given social formation are not all simply clones from some master model of
the dominant ideology. (1) If a mode of production is seen as creating the
conditions for related ideological modes whose function is to interpellate
subjects to fit the dominant relations of production, then the concept of social
formation allows us to conceive a structure of varying ideological determinants. The existence of various positions within this ideological configuration
provides for the possibility of differing modes of interpellation which are more
or less determined—unified—by the dominant ideology. (2) Each ISA is
marked internally by class struggle and thus contains within itself the
possibility of dysfunction. And (3) the particular nature of the ISAs—familial,

religious, educational, etc.—provides for the possibility of nonclass determinations in the interpellation of subjects.

While the function of the dominant ideology is to unify the heterogeneous
determinations of the different ISAs—"despite its diversity and contradictions," Althusser claims—that unity is subject to the shifting relationship of forces which results from class and nonclass struggles. (Since Althusser does not deal directly with nonclass determinants, I am depending on the
work of Ernesto Laclau and Chantal Mouffe for this insight. Laclau: "This
unity can, of course, be disarticulated and recomposed by other discourses. In
this sense, the subjectivity of the social agents as such is constantly changing
because it's not a homogeneous subjectivity but a constantly recreated unity
depending on the whole relation of forces in a society at a given moment"
["Recasting Marxism," 100].)

In a different vocabulary, what we are talking about here is dissemination.
And Laclau's use of the term "discourse" provides for a convenient shift from
a discussion of the subject to one of the politics of language. For, due to a
happy reversal, the explanatory power of the linguistic model for a conception of politics also offers a political model for a conception of language. And
here I can do no better than summarize Lewis's important discussion in
"Reference and Dissemination." I begin with a quotation:

> . . . if it is once allowed that conflict (and, hence, domination) may occur in the
> social use of signs (it is clear that Derrida allows this), it no longer can be claimed
> that the value of signs are equally unsecured (it seems to me that sometimes
> Derrida claims this and sometimes not). In this respect, some deconstructionists
> purchase alleged grounds for epistemological uncertainty precisely at the cost of
> obscuring the role of social power in the process of fixing and disseminating
> references. (p. 40)

Reference, then, is to be seen as the result of a conflictual social process in
which various interests compete with one another in order to assign particular values to particular signs. While in the abstract we can agree with Saussure
that signification is due to the value accorded to a term in the differential
environment of language, Lewis suggests that we must go on to ask where
that value itself comes from. The answer lies in part in Umberto Eco's insight
that "the referent of a term can only be a *cultural unit*" (*A Theory of Semiotics*,
68). These cultural units, furthermore, draw their value from their placement
within language's "multidimensional network of metonymies, each of which
is explained by a cultural convention rather than by an original resemblance"
(*The Role of the Reader*, 78). Reference results not from a one-to-one correspondence between a concept and a thing but through the culturally determined placement and displacement of the concept along a metonymic
chain of sign functions. And the same is true for metaphor: a metaphor does
not simply substitute one concept for another according to a scheme of
resemblance; the terms sit in adjacent chains. Metaphor, then, is the effect of

a rapid displacement of intermediary terms which connect one chain with the other. Metaphor, in other words, is an effect of metonymy. Reference and metaphor occur because of a metonymic displacement of frames, a process Derrida refers to as dissemination.

What has all this to do with politics? Lewis writes, "What is at stake in the program of dissemination, then, is the exact possibility of *consuming* cultural products in an effectively *different* way . . . [through a process which] works on the basis of elaborating new metonymical relations between texts by shifting the contexts that enable such texts to acquire references" (p. 54). The social context we are speaking of here (to return briefly to Althusser's ISA essay) is the class struggle. The class which gains control over the process of dissemination—the class which succeeds in securing the reference of concepts in a way that best serves its interests—is the class with the ruling ideology. Using Althusser's terminology from *For Marx* this process could be described as the epistemological break (Derrida's "scission") which establishes the substitution of one problematic for another.

I wish to sum up this portion of my discussion with two more quotations from Lewis before turning to the practice of some Language poets:

> If it is remembered that Althusser separates the object of knowledge from the real object and that he views the validity of a theoretical discourse as a function of its discursive systemization and effectivity, then what these passages convey is precisely an understanding of concepts as "tropic-concepts," that is, as discursive operations that provisionally enable one to accomplish specific tasks by activating various series of metonymical chains in and for specific circumstances. (p. 50)

> I believe that Althusser—in his heart of hearts, of course—generally considers not only that concepts are metaphors in and for theory but also that concepts are to be understood as operating metonymically so as to move the users of concepts along specific interpretantial chains in order that they may arrive at a specific place and perform a specific act. . . . (p. 49)

So how can a particular poetic practice serve as an ideology critique? We first must define ideology critique as a mode of investigation. Fredric Jameson refers to this mode as Marxism's "negative hermeneutic," dramatically exemplified by Walter Benjamin's famous statement that "there is no document of civilization which is not at one and the same time a document of barbarism" (*Political Unconscious*, 286). Jameson explains that such an investigative mode begins with the assumption that:

> the ideological function of mass culture is understood as a process whereby otherwise dangerous and protopolitical impulses are "managed" and defused, rechanneled and offered spurious objects. . . . [Nevertheless] this process cannot be grasped as one of sheer violence (the theory of hegemony is explicitly distinguished from control by brute force) nor as one inscribing the appropriate

attitudes upon a blank slate, but must necessarily involve a complex strategy of rhetorical persuasion in which substantial incentives are offered for ideological adherence. (p. 287)

All ideology critique, I should add, is in this sense "functionalist." What would a Marxism look like that did not in one form or another operate according to this negative hermeneutic? It is the "blank slate" conception of ideology mentioned above that is attributed to Althusser's conception of ideology and indeed is "functionalist" in its more restricted sense. But, as I have strived to point out, Althusser's conception should be characterized more as the imposition of frames (problematics) which provide the field of reference for particular terms or impulses. Althusser's notion of symptomatic reading is in this sense the attempt to intuit the frames which accord value (ideological charge) to concepts within them. In this general sense his own practice of ideology critique resembles that put forward by Peter Burger (who in this instance draws on the work of Herbert Marcuse): "When one refers to the function of an individual work, one generally speaks figuratively; for the consequences that one may obserye or infer are not primarily a function of its special qualities but rather of the manner which regulates the commerce with works of this kind in a given society or in certain strata or classes of a society. I have chosen the term 'institution of art' to characterize such framing conditions" (*Theory of the Avant-Garde*, 12).

Some Language poetry must be seen as operating precisely within this mode of attention to the framing conditions of the "institution of art." This poetic practice, of course, does not provide readings of individual works but instead explores the function of frames in general, the process by which "dangerous and protopolitical impulses" tend to be neutralized and subverted within the hegemonic conception of art today. While these poets deny that a particular poetic "style" or mode *a priori* carries any specific political charge, they nevertheless insist that certain modes are more easily appropriated into the dominant ideology than are others. Poetic practice thus must be seen as a form of class struggle.

Language poet Ron Silliman writes for example, in "Disappearance of the Word, Appearance of the World," that "the social function of the language arts, especially the poem, place[s] them in an important position to carry the class struggle *for* consciousness to the level *of* consciousness" (*The L=A=N=G=U=A=G=E Book*, 131; cited hereafter as *LB*). If the sign is "an arena of the class struggle," as V. N. Volosinov suggests (*Marxism and the Philosophy of Language*, 23), then there may be a great deal at stake in a disseminatory practice. Poet Charles Bernstein points out that another part of the answer is a poetry that "bares the frame," as the Russian Formalists would put it. Because our experiences are structured through their syntactical arrangement, a poetry that bares its own construction can serve as a "syntactical exploration of consciousness" (*LB,* 43). In general, Language poets such as Silliman, Bernstein, Lyn Hejinian, Bruce Andrews, and Barrett Watten often structure their poetry so as to draw our attention to the politics of the production of reference, the subject, and the "closed" text.

(This is not to suggest, we should note here, that all those poets labeled as Language poets share a single political position. Watten, for instance, has frequently criticized the notion, so often associated with "Language" writing *per se,* that referential language is reified language. Other poets, such as Robert Grenier and Clark Coolidge, insist on distinguishing their positions not only from the Reference-Equals-Reification argument [to be explained below] but from any form of Marxism whatsoever. Consequently, any analysis of the political tendencies of Language writers has to respect their heterogeneity, and to specify which poet can be associated with which political stance. Furthermore, the political claims of individual poets have varied over the last ten to fifteen years, making it necessary to take such changes into account.)

In "Stray Straws and Straw Men" Bernstein lists the major assumptions behind the complaints against Language poetry. Work such as Silliman's, Bernstein states, "may discomfort those who want a poetry of personal communication, flowing freely from the inside with the words of a natural rhythm of life, lived daily" (*LB,* 39). Behind such discomfort often is the belief that poetry should be honest, direct, authentic, artless, sincere, spontaneous, expressive, *natural.* In such a view of poetry, Bernstein explains in the introduction to his *Paris Review* anthology, "communication is schematized as a two-way wire with the message shuttling back and forth in blissful ignorance of the (its) transom (read: ideology)"; the message passes between two "terminal points (me→you)." Subjects are simple, meaning exists "out there" waiting to be communicated, and texts should be neutral, natural, transparent. In short, the assumptions behind such poetry, as we shall see, are the basic assumptions of bourgeois subjectivity.

One Language school argument counter to the above is that reference is a form of reification. In the essay "Reification and the Consciousness of the Proletariat" Georg Lukács offers the following definition of reification: "Its basis is that a relation between people takes on the character of a thing and thus acquires a 'phantom objectivity', an autonomy that seems so strictly rational and all-embracing as to conceal every trace of its fundamental nature: the relation between people" (*History and Class Consciousness,* 83). By analogy some Language writers claim that the same process applies to the production of language and poetry. Signifiers here replace the commodity and reference replaces surplus value. Reference is thus to be seen as the end result of the social process of language production, not as the inherent quality of the words themselves. Like Lewis, some Language poets add a Marxist twist to Saussure's theory by insisting that the social context determines which particular signifieds may relate to a given signifier. Ignoring the social relations inscribed within the signifier, then, is analogous to ignoring the social relations within the commodity. "Grammatically centered meaning," poet Steve McCaffery claims, "is meaning realized through a specific mode of temporalization. It is understood as postponed reward at the end (the culmination) of a series of syntagms. It is that fetish in which the sentence completes itself. Meaning is like capital in so far as it extends its law of value to new objects. Like surplus value, meaning is frequently 'achieved' to be reinvested in the extending chain of significations. This is seen quite clearly in classical narrative, where meaning operates as accumulated and accumulative units in the furtherance of 'plot' or 'character development': those elements of representation which lead to a destination outside the domain of the signifier" (*LB*, 160).

Silliman, again in "Disappearance of the Word, Appearance of the World"—the title referring to the goal of realism, the word's disappearance from consciousness as it draws forth its referent—explains that the language of earlier modes of poetry or of present tribal literatures is "felt," its nonsemantic physical characteristics foregrounded in various ways (rhyme, "nonsense syllables," variant spellings). But attention to the physicality of the medium has increasingly disappeared in Western language over the past two centuries. Silliman writes:

> What happens when language moves toward and passes into a capitalist stage of development is an anaesthetic transformation of the perceived tangibility of the word, with corresponding increases in its descriptive and narrative capacities, preconditions for the invention of "realism," the optical illusion in capital-ist thought. These developments are tied directly to the nature of reference in language, which under capitalism is transformed (deformed) into referentiality. (*LB*, 125)

Realism's valorization of reference, Silliman claims, obscures the social relationships inhering in the poem and thus contributes to the overall process of reification. It is to the ruling class's benefit that we do not recognize the socially-constructed nature of language, for if we did we might realize that the hegemonic views of reality—such as that commodities are "natural"—are to a certain extent arbitrary and, therefore, open to questioning. Silliman favors a poetry, then, that foregrounds its "gesturality"—the traces of its sociality, its constructedness—and explores the limits of its medium: that is, language.

The following passage from Lyn Hejinian's *Writing Is an Aid to Memory* (1978) may illustrate such foregrounding:

we are parting with description
termed blue may be perfectly blue
goats do have damp noses
that test and now I dine drinking with
others
adult blue butterfly for a swim with cheerful birds

I suppose we hear a muddle of rhythms in water
bond vegetables binder thereof for thread
and no crisp fogs
                                    spice quilt mix
                        know shipping pivot
                                    sprinkle with a little melody
                        nor blot past this dot mix
                        now for a bit and fog of bath rain
        do dot goats

Many poetic assumptions and techniques are called into question here
(although not dispensed with): lineation, enjambment, syntax, reference,
rhyme, rhythm, alliteration, repetition, point of view, and voice. The first line,
for example, comments on the appropriateness of reference, implying that
description—the method of realism—is no longer necessary or viable (we do
not know which). Without the end punctuation, we read on through the line
break, where another question arises: Is the second line a continuation of the
first or a discrete unit? The first line may stand by itself as methodological
statement, or "termed" may refer back to description. But that possibility is
challenged as line two progresses, appearing now as separate from the first, a
fragment with no clear connection to the first line. We may read the line as a
sentence *in media res,* the beginning and perhaps the end of the sentence seen
as erased from view. And what do goats with damp noses have to do with
either of the previous lines? Line four provides a possible answer: what is in
question here seems to be the possibility of description, whether something
called "blue" can be "perfectly blue," whether we can justify descriptions by
recourse to the physical world—touching the goats' noses and agreeing that
they are indeed damp. Line four, then, links these lines provisionally to the
theme of proof, of the adequacy of language to match experiences through a
series of tests. Those tests rest on social convention, however, proving ade-
quate only insofar as they meet some communal standard. "That test and now
I dine drinking with/ others": the coherence as written here overrides the
significance of the enjambment between the "I" and the "other," the distance
that separates the subject from any complete communion with the object
except as they are mediated through sociality.

Such a reading, however, seems to break down as the poem continues.
Sociality in line five now takes on a sinister sense, the naive butterfly swim-
ming among what seem to be cheerful birds; but if looks prove deceiving—as
the previous lines on description suggest—then the butterfly is in trouble. The
sixth line shifts to another narrative frame, apparently following through with
the water reference of line five. But "bond vegetables binder thereof for
thread"? All narrative or thematic coherence between the lines appears to
break down here, only to recur fleetingly in "and no crisp fogs," another
comment on description. Unless, of course, "crips" functions as a noun rather
than an adjective, and "fogs" as a verb rather than a noun. The progression of

the poem so far does not privilege such a reading, but neither does it prevent it, especially when we read "spice quilt mix." Is this a series of nouns? An elliptical command: "[You] spice [the] quilt mix"? Such a grammatical pattern shows up in the next line, "know shipping pivot." However we choose to read the poem, whatever its thematics, the form of the poem and its demands on the reader force the issue of construction, of language as a conflictual process of arranging material units.

In addition to the critique of common assumptions about reference, much so-called Language poetry also engages in the current debate over the status of the *cogito* or subject. Poetry, then, which functions according to the notion of the poet/speaker as an independent subject who, having "found his voice," presents a situation seen from a single point of view, fosters the key ideological concept of bourgeois society: the self-sufficient, self-determined individual free to participate in the marketplace. The standard poetic notions of voice, expression, intention, point-of-view, etc., must therefore come under close scrutiny in any materialist poetic. In his book-length poem, *a.k.a.*, Bob Perelman makes such a critique of the subject the content of his work:

> I is to other as shopping is to Christmas. An immense pressure to locate the bargains amid the sense of betrayed values. One by one, I took her hand and led her and was carried upstairs. Goodnight thousands of times, until inside and outside have the identical awesome echo. Stories settle down comfortably from interstellar distances. Naturally enough I reach for warmth. No shame in being a rock, a tree, a person inside perspective and thus a bit foreshortened. Ceaseless repetition stimulated chemistry. He ate what was in front of him, swallowing the implications. (p. 24)

In this passage the "I" plays many grammatical roles, none of them being granted any primacy. The I in the first sentence is already in the position of the other, the third person, serving as a noun rather than as a shifter substituting for a speaker. Lacan asks, "Is the place that I occupy as the subject of a signifier concentric or eccentric, in relation to the place I occupy as subject of the signified?" (*Ecrits*, 165). The speaker can only speak of herself through the mediated distance of a word, "I," and consequently never can unify the I that is spoken of and the I that speaks. Through the economy of desire the self submits to being other in order to be at all. As Michael Palmer has written in correspondence, the imagination can be seen in this context as the manifestation of desire, the force of "dis-placement" that produces not the monad but the heterogeneous (Letter to George Hartley, 6 November 1986).

Perelman, in his talk "The First Person," associates the traditional "voice" poem—such as William Stafford's "Travelling Through the Dark"—with the closed text, in which the "poet is firmly in the driver's seat, '*I* could hear the wilderness,' and firmly in control of the meaning, '*I* thought hard for us all.' . . . here, the I is in a privileged position, unaffected by the words" ("The First

Person," 156). Perelman contrasts such a poem with the text which "insists on the reader participating," the open text, which Hejinian defines as follows:

> The open text, by definition, is open to the world and particularly to the reader. It invites participation, rejects the authority of the writer over the reader and thus, by analogy, the authority implicit in other (social, economic, cultural) hierarchies. It speaks for writing that is generative rather than directive. . . . The open text often emphasizes or foregrounds process, either the process of the original composition or of subsequent compositions by readers, and thus resists the cultural tendencies that seek to identify and fix material, turn it into a product; that is, it resists reduction and commodification. ("The Rejection of Closure," 272)

Hejinian locates the danger of commodification not so much in reference as in the view of the text as product rather than as process. Though it may sound contradictory, the foregrounding of the materiality of the language, the revelation of the word's objecthood (so to speak), draws attention to the process of language, the manipulation of material units within the signifying chain in such a way so as to create meaning. Meaning exists within an active inter-agential process rather than as an object or product existing outside of language, just as value results from a social process rather than from some inherent quality of the object. Such attention is helpful in reading the following passage from Steve Benson's "On Time in Another Place":

> They go to a foreign country to have a talk. A forest
>
> for example, Wales, Cambodia, it doesn't matter so long as
>
> givens are posited at an angle oblique enough to their assump-
>   A woman and her daughter both wear sweaters buttoned
> tions that the situation appeals mostly to their sensations
> halfway up the front, black and navy blue respectively. A
> and their identities are inapparent, up for grabs or subject
> man on a pale green motor-scooter wears a slightly darker,
> to the oblivion of their absorption in the not-there: imagination
> deeper colored sweater of about the same tint. Walking
> memories, possibilities, et cetera. The irrelevancy of such
> between her husband and her young son, a woman whose dress is
> residual impressions, which seem to ride loose bubbles of
> blazoned with broad magenta-pink and green and blue and white
> hot air rising to expel them via speech, disperses them too
> stripes has an unfastened button-down long-sleeved pastel
> easily, whether or not words want to press them to explosion.
> sweater on over it. . . .

The "desire to say," as Hejinian puts it, leads to the superimposition of narratives, the attempt to speak everything at once. Such a writing process emphasizes the singularity and limitation of narration while acceding to the necessity of narration. The two narratives in Benson's poem continually merge and retract, seeking points of synthesis while rejecting any total synthesis, much as in Benson's book, *Blindspots*. In a review of the latter book Carla Harryman writes, "The blindspots, the words that stand out as holes, 'stress the act.' . . . The possibility of continual transformation inspires insatiable desire. . . . The finesse is that one anticipates the empty spaces will be filled. But Benson, restlessly dissatisfied with his product, the completed detail, constantly alters the way any next thing comes into being. He places his own agility under attack, which psychological strategy encourages the work in its mutations. This too fuels the desiring machine" ("What In Fact Was Originally Improvised," 73).

As we have seen, the work of these poets is in part a reaction against the assumptions about reference, the subject, and textual closure that lie, in their view, behind the dominant poetic discourse. The disjunction, discontinuity, and indeterminacy of many of the poems I have been discussing grow out of a critique of bourgeois ideology which is seen to inform much contemporary poetic practice. But is this enough to challenge the reifying effects of the dominant conceptions about language? Or is this poetic mode itself a sign of reification, its fragmentary form resulting from a rejection of the very social process of meaning-production that these poets claim to foreground? The answer to either question, I would argue, depends more on the social and aesthetic context in which such a poetic mode appears than on any supposed inherent value of the mode itself. "The identification of reference," Watten writes, "and of normative grammar behind that, with the commodification of language might be true in a given time and place. For example, the French bourgeois education Breton received probably approached this kind of social coding. But writers in the present would be lucky to have the lids on that tight" (*Total Syntax*, 54). However tight the lids might now be (or, in other words, however tightly controlled the possibilities of language might be), the important point here is that the political effects of form depend on historical context. While Breton's opening up of poetic form might have been an effective response in the repressive context of early-twentieth century France, the American poet's abandonment of control, Watten suggests, may only contribute to an already anarchic environment with no signs of control from above or from anywhere else. Thus Watten has said, "I don't see that an open text, one that isn't organized around content, doesn't run similar kinds of risks [of creating a power imbalance between writer and reader] in terms of overcoding or blanking out (undercoding)" ("Barrett Watten on Poetry and Politics," 199).

Poet Bruce Andrews's own practice grows out of the desire to lay bare the social coding that shapes our present use of language. Andrews hopes to *extend* the production of meaning, not to deny it. Such a position lies behind the following passage from one of his poems:

gaps

shocks through

absorbing

hover

the subjunctive

we're

less

thoughts

(*Wobbling*, 80)

Even though the standard syntactical patterns and grammatical units are missing here, this poem nevertheless can mean and can be read. Andrews has opened up the possibilities of syntax, allowing the reader to determine the paths she will pursue in combining these words into a meaningful complex. If one were to draw lines from each unit to other units close by, as in a connect-the-dots puzzle, then one might visualize the various possible combinations offered above. In any case, the poem lays bare the device of standard syntax, revealing its arbitrary and socially-determined nature.

Andrews explains this practice of baring the frame as follows:

> Laying bare the device remains as a task but it becomes a more social act, of social unbalancing, of a social reflexivity of content, rather than some kind of (what I have called in the past) preppie formalism. Because the modernism that's at stake now is more public and is more involved with the conditions of meaning, it also becomes more social. So that if people are arguing (as some of the post-structuralists seem to) that social meaning has disappeared, then just trying to disrupt the system with some radical formalism isn't going to be enough. Instead, if something's going to be disruptive, or disrupted, it's going to have to be *method*, seen in a more social sense—as the social organization of signs, as ideology, as discourse; those are the more broadly social things that need to be shaken up: historicized, politicized, contextualized, totalized—by laying bare the social devices, or the social rules which are at work. ("Total Equals What: Poetics & Praxis," 57; italics in original)

Andrews emphasizes that he sees his work not just as technique for technique's sake, but as a materialist critique of the present social forces which encode our day-to-day language practice. Such a poetry functions as an ideology critique. Such a questioning closely parallels Althusser's reexamination of the connections between language, ideology, and the self: "Like all obviousnesses, including those that make a word 'name a thing' or 'have a meaning' (therefore including the obviousness of the 'transparency' of language), the 'obviousness' that you and I are subjects—and that that does not cause any problems—is an ideological effect" (*Lenin,* 171–72). In their questioning of the function of reference, the self-sufficiency of the subject, and the adherence to standard syntax of the closed text, some so-called Language poets have developed a poetry which functions not as ornamentation or as self-expression, but as a baring of the frames of bourgeois ideology itself.

THREE

Jameson's Perelman

Reification and the
Material Signifier

In *New Left Review* 146 (July–August 1984) Fredric Jameson published his by now notorious essay "Postmodernism, or the Cultural Logic of Late Capitalism." In that essay he compares Lacan's description of schizophrenic language to the writings of the Language poets. He points out in particular that Bob Perelman, in his poem "China," seems to have made schizophrenic language the basis of his aesthetic. Prior to Jameson, John Ensslin, in an essay entitled "Schizophrenic Writing," which appeared in $L=A=N=G=U=A=G=E$ 1.4 (August 1978), also pointed out the striking similarities between clinical accounts of schizophrenic language and recent poetry, but he offered "one precaution: don't confuse schizophrenic speech with poetic language. . . . to treat [schizophrenic speech] as a freakish bit of literature is to overlook the fact that these bizarre turns of language are the products of a torturous state of mind." Jameson's problem, I will argue, is the opposite of this—confusing poetic language with schizophrenic speech.

To be sure, Jameson is careful to explain that he is using Lacan's account only as a useful description, not to imply that Perelman is in any way a clinical schizophrenic. But even if such is the case—I will later argue against his claim to innocent description—the usefulness of such a comparison is far from obvious, *especially* in the way he uses it. Nevertheless, the positive value of the Lacanian notion of schizophrenia, if there is one in this context, is its bringing into focus two conflicting accounts of the effects of reification on language use, as well as two conflicting aesthetics. At the heart of the debate is the material signifier—the significatory unit (whether the phoneme, the word, the phrase, or the sentence) which has been isolated from standard syntactical patterns, drawing attention to itself as much as, or more than, to any concept it may point to. The question comes down to this: What are the political effects of the use of the material signifier?

Before directly addressing this question, however, we must reconstruct Jameson's argument as it leads to his discussion of Perelman. One reason for this is that, although I believe Jameson's comparison has obvious problems, his approach to periodization nevertheless demands our attention. The key to evaluating Jameson's comments about postmodernism is to grasp the basic concept behind his division of cultural history into periods. That concept, based on Nicos Poulantzas's extension of Althusserian theory, is social formation.

In *Political Power and Social Classes* Poulantzas writes that the "mode of production constitutes an abstract-formal object which does not exist in the strong sense of reality. . . . The only thing which really exists is a historically determined social formation, i.e. a social whole, in the widest sense, at a given moment in its historical existence; e.g. France under Louis Bonaparte, England during the Industrial Revolution" (p. 15). "Mode of production" is to be viewed as a methodological concept, not as some real discrete object. The social formation may ultimately be determined by a mode of production but can never be reduced to one. Poulantzas explains further that "a social formation . . . presents a particular combination, a specific overlapping of several 'pure' modes of production. . . . Bismarck's Germany is characterized by a specific combination of capitalist, feudal and patriarchal modes of production whose combination alone exists in the strong sense of the term, . . . a social formation historically determined as a particular object." The point to develop here is the expanded view of historical determination that Poulantzas explains as follows: "The dominance of one mode of production over others in a social formation causes the matrix of this mode of production . . . to mark the whole of the formation. In this way a historically determined social formation is specified by a particular articulation (through an index of dominance and overdetermination) of its different economic, political, ideological and theoretical levels or instances" (pp. 15–16).

The key phrase in the above passage is "index of dominance and over-determination." Rather than crudely reduce the complex network of various social determinations to the economic, we can now take into account the influences of many relatively autonomous levels or instances at one time, each level's relative autonomy stemming from its own determined placement within a network of competing modes of production. Raymond Williams refers to these competing influences as the residual (the remaining influence of past modes), the dominant, and the emergent (nascent modes struggling for dominance) (*Marxism and Literature*, 121–27). One problem we avoid, at least in part, by focusing on the particularity and relative autonomy of the various levels of the social formation is the positing of homologies between different levels. The Hegelian notion of an expressive totality—in which each analytically distinguished level of society is seen as an expression of some essence and thus structurally similar to all other levels—often leads to the conclusion that cultural objects are expressions of the economic base. This is not to say that the Althusserians reject the concept of totality, just that they define it differently. "The structure is not an essence *outside* the economic phenomena," Althusser explains, " which comes and alters their aspect, forms and relations and which is effective on them as an absent cause, *absent because it is outside them. The absence of the cause in the structure's 'metonymic causality' on its effects is not the fault of the exteriority of the structure with respect to the economic phenomena; on the contrary, it is the very form of the interiority of the structure . . . in its effects"* (Althusser, 188; italics in original).

The reasons for this lengthy discussion of the Althusserian concept of social formation should become clear when we now turn to Jameson's notion of a cultural dominant in his definition of postmodernism. Whether we agree with his definition is, for the moment, beside the point; the particular way he frames this question is in any case of great value. From the concept of social formation Jameson develops an important analogy on the cultural plane—which we presumably could call the *cultural formation*—an analogy that becomes clear when Jameson writes that "it seems to me essential to grasp 'postmodernism' not as a style, but rather as a cultural dominant: a conception which allows for the presence and coexistence of a range of very different, yet subordinate features" ("Postmodernism," 56). Once he substitutes cultural dominant for structural dominant (or "structure-in-dominance"), the rest of the analogy falls into place, the cultural formation being seen as determined by the various conflicting cultural modes of production at a given moment. After doing so, he can then (theoretically, at least) avoid many of the problems that surround all attempts at periodization, especially the problem of explaining how, for instance, an artist from what we determine to be the modern period can look quite like those artists we associate with an earlier or later period, just as the concept of social formation helps to explain the existence of typically feudal features in, for example, the capitalist era. The notion of cultural dominant thus explains the coexistence of various artistic modes during the period Jameson calls postmodern: "I am very far from feeling that all cultural production today is 'postmodern' in the broad sense I will be conferring on this term. The postmodern is however the force field in which very different kinds of cultural impulses— . . . 'residual' and 'emergent' forms of cultural production—must make their way" (p. 57).

Such a formula allows him to write, for example, that "Gertrude Stein, Raymond Roussel, or Marcel Duchamp . . . may be considered outright postmodernists, *avant la lettre*" (p. 56). He goes on to qualify this statement, however, in what may be the most important point in his essay: "What has not been taken into account by this view is . . . the social position of the older modernism" (p. 56). "[Modernism and postmodernism] still remain utterly distinct in their meaning and social function, owing to the very different positioning of postmodernism in the economic system of late capital, and beyond that, to the transformation of the very sphere of culture in contemporary society" (p. 57). Literary form, in other words, takes on its particular political meaning from its position within a specific historical context. Having said this, however, Jameson then greatly overgeneralizes the political context of postmodernism, neglecting to sort out the various contexts which Poulantzas's conception of social formation posits. The social positioning of a particular form may have a different political charge depending on its relationship not only to the period but also to its overdetermined location within the social formation. (We should note here that whether Language poetry can be called the cultural dominant remains to be seen—see Lee Bartlett's "What Is 'Language Poetry' " and Silliman's "The Political Economy of Poetry.")

As I have just suggested, it is when Jameson fleshes out this very promising outline by describing what he sees as the political effects of postmodernism in the present social formation that problems arise, most notably a return to the very homologies that he has elsewhere warned us against. More specifically, his importation of Lacan's discussion of schizophrenia leads him to the traditional Marxist denunciation of modernist (and now postmodernist) fragmentation, rather than to an appreciation of Perelman's particular use of the material signifier as a political critique. Jameson frames his discussion of Perelman's "China" in such a way that he prematurely forecloses any other avenues of a more positive analysis. That frame begins with his discussion of what he sees as the constitutive feature of postmodernism: its new depthlessness.

By contrasting Van Gogh's painting of the peasant shoes with Andy Warhol's "Diamond Dust Shoes" Jameson illustrates one of the major differences he sees between modernism and postmodernism. While according to Jameson Van Gogh's shoes must be seen as the result of the reification of the senses—in this case, sight—due to the increased division of labor under capitalism, Jameson also draws attention to its Utopian side, in which "the most glorious materialization of pure colour in oil paint is to be seen as . . . an act of compensation" (p. 59) for precisely that fragmented life in capitalist society. The painting speaks to us, imparts its meaning as it "draws the whole absent world and earth into revelation around itself," representing the wretched life of the peasant woman. The problem with Warhol's shoes, however, is that they do not speak to us at all. Instead "we have a random collection of dead objects, hanging together on the canvas like so many turnips, as shorn of their earlier life-world as the pile of shoes left over at Auschwitz, or the remainders and tokens of some incomprehensible and tragic fire in a packed dancehall" (p. 60). Note that the images of Auschwitz and a tragic fire are not incidental here. Even though Jameson has just stressed the need to see the Utopian value of Van Gogh's reified impressionism, he expends very little of such dialectical thought on his postmodern examples. Although later in the essay he will try to rescue his argument from a "pre-Marxian" moralism, it remains clear here that Warhol *ought* to do something other than present dead and meaningless objects on a canvas.

At any rate, this passage from Van Gogh to Warhol, Jameson claims, illustrates "perhaps the supreme formal feature" of postmodernism—its anti-hermeneutical, superficial depthlessness. The "deep" works of the modernists have been succeeded by the slick TV surfaces of the simulacrum, the image. Jameson describes one problem with the simulacrum as follows:

the simulacrum['s] . . . particular function lies in what Sartre would have called the *derealization* of the whole surrounding world of everyday reality. Your moment of doubt and hesitation as to the breath and warmth of [Duane Hanson's] polyester figures, in other words, tends to return upon the real human beings moving about you in the museum, and to transform them also for the briefest instant into so many dead and flesh-coloured simulacra in their own right. The world thereby momentarily loses its depth and threatens to become a glossy skin, a stereoscopic illusion, a rush of filmic images without density. ("Postmodernism," 76–77)

The simulacrum's derealization of everyday life affects not only spatial but temporal depth as well. Jameson argues that "what was once, in the historical novel as Lukács defines it, the organic genealogy of the bourgeois collective project . . . has meanwhile itself become a vast collection of images, a multitudinous photographic simulacrum. . . . In faithful conformity to poststructuralist linguistic theory, the past as 'referent' finds itself gradually bracketed, and then effaced altogether, leaving us with nothing but texts" (p. 66). Postmodernists substitute a nostalgic cannibalization of past styles for an older attempt to come to terms with "real" history. This crisis in historicity, he claims, appears in a formal innovation of postmodernism, namely the transformation of the time-bound narrative sentence into the "finished, complete, and isolated punctual event-objects which find themselves sundered from any present situation" (p. 70)—the material signifier.

In order to make sense of these "heaps of fragments," Jameson next resorts to Lacan's account of schizophrenia "as a breakdown in the signifying chain, that is, the interlocking syntagmatic series of signifiers which constitutes an utterance or a meaning" (p. 71–72). The function of the sentence is to form our personal identity: "If we are unable to unify the past, present, and future of the sentence," Jameson claims, "then we are similarly unable to unify the past, present, and future of our own biographical experience or psychic life: (p. 72). (The key word here which he seems to ignore in his analysis is "unable.") The point Jameson makes here—that makes all this relevant for Marxism—is that the meaningful grasp of historical time is necessary for political praxis. Without it we cannot recognize the historical determination of present conditions which we need to change. But it is Jameson's extension of all this to cultural production to which I object.

My first objection is that his description of the signifying chain does not convey the full import of Lacan's conception of it. Lacan is not talking about individual sentences when he uses this term, although sentences do illustrate on a manifest level what he is describing; rather, "signifying chain" refers to the structure of the unconscious as a whole, which can be compared to a sentence but cannot be reduced to one. (I am not suggesting that Jameson does not know this, only that he does not make this clear—see his "Imaginary and Symbolic in Lacan.") "That the dream uses speech makes no difference," Lacan writes, "since for the unconscious it is only one among several elements of the representation" (Lacan, *Ecrits*, 161).

The signifying chain, Lacan claims, constitutes the unconscious itself. But this occurs only after the primal repression of the Imaginary phase, a phase of primary narcissism during which the subject cannot distinguish its own body from that of others, seeing instead "a world of bodies and organs which in some fashion lacks a phenomenological center and a privileged point of view" (Jameson, "Imaginary and Symbolic in Lacan," 354). The failure to complete this process of repression leads to the various forms of psychosis. Lacan refers to this failure as the *foreclusion* or foreclosure of the Other, the refusal or inability to enter the Symbolic Order of signification. "Foreclosure effects neither the judgment of existence nor the negation; only the symbol remains, but, because of the absence of its relation to the signified, it loses its true value as a signifier, as a symbol. It is no longer any more than an image taken for reality. The imaginary has become the real" (Lemaire, *Jacques Lacan,* 233). In other words, the schizophrenic is left with material signifiers. (This description of the image taken for reality reveals the connection behind Jameson's association of the simulacrum and schizophrenia, a point that becomes important when he discusses "China.")

According to Lacan, schizophrenic discourse is binary while Symbolic discourse is ternary. The schizophrenic remains at or reverts to the Imaginary state of unmediated fusion of self and other, of subject and signifier. Only in the Symbolic Order do these two poles become mediated by a third—language. There is no meaning engendered by the schizophrenic's material signifier; the question arises, however, of whether such is the case with the poet's material signifier. In other words, does the poet's signifier signify? This question brings me to my second and major complaint against Jameson's use of "schizophrenic" even as a descriptive term (although it is obviously more than a descriptive term for Jameson). There is a world of difference between the schizophrenic's *inability* to get beyond the material signifier and the artist's deliberate reduction to one: whereas the schizophrenic could be said to operate on a pre-Symbolic level of discourse, poets, such as Perelman, operate on a meta-Symbolic plane. Jameson implies that the effect of the material signifier, whether produced by the psychotic or the artist, is the same in either case. But in order to reach this conclusion, he has to ignore his own argument about the variability of formal effect within different contexts.

I would argue that Jameson's brief commentary on "China" does not constitute his analysis of the poem. The actual analysis of "China" and, by illegitimate extension, of all Language writing lies in his inserting the poem at a specific moment in his essay. Although Jameson claims that he mainly wants to show that "schizophrenic" writing has no necessary relationship to psychosis, the momentum of the essay necessitates just that relationship; adopting the Lacanian apparatus at such a key moment in the essay is not merely descriptive but ascriptive. The use of the label "schizophrenia," in other words, is no innocent gesture but instead a strategic form of guilt-by-association.

Now to Jameson's discussion of "China." "Many things," he begins, "could be said about this interesting exercise in discontinuities: not the least paradoxical is the reemergence here across these disjoined sentences of some more unified global meaning" (p. 74). (This may seem less paradoxical to Perelman, who has written that there "is no such thing as nonnarrative writing" ["Exchangeable Frames," 168].) Jameson goes on to say that the poem "does seem to capture something of the excitement of the immense, unfinished social experiment of the New China." The important unstated point is that the charge of schizophrenia may not hold here because of this reemergent unity. But Jameson next assures us that "we have not thereby fully exhausted the structural secrets of Perelman's poem, which turns out to have little enough to do with the referent called China" (p. 75). Pointing out that Perelman's lines in the poem were written as captions to photographs in a Chinese book, Jameson contends that the unity of the poem lies outside it in the absent Chinese text. Perelman's poem is thus a text about a text, just as photorealist works are pictures of pictures, or simulacra.

Once Perelman's poem becomes reduced to the simulacrum, it has the same political effect for Jameson as the schizophrenic signifier. In both cases we confront free-floating signifiers with little or no connection to the "real world," serving at best as decoration, but more often more negatively as a negative distraction from the real work to be done, a symptom and perpetuation of the reification brought on by capitalism. But there seems to be a naive mimetism at work here that exposes the problem behind Jameson's attack on the simulacrum. Is the authenticity or political efficacy of a work really dependent on the immediacy of its model? And are a text's model and its referent identical? How Perelman generated his text is in any case irrelevant to our understanding it. Jameson here resembles Plato's attack on the poet for creating a copy of a copy.

Using Ernest Mandel's conception of Late Capitalism, or the period of multinational capital which has transformed society into a "whole new decentred global network" beyond representation, Jameson posits that the corresponding technological analogue is the machine of reproduction—the television, the camera, the computer—whose processes are also beyond representation. The modernist artists, excited by the "sculptural nodes of energy" of the electric and combustion motors (machines of *pro*duction), represented that kinetic energy in their art. But postmodernists, Jameson continues, are more concerned with "the processes of reproduction, . . . [such as] movie cameras, video, tape recorders, the whole technology of the production and reproduction of the simulacrum" (p. 79).

Depending on how it is used, such a formula of homological relations could become a technologism and a Marxism at its crudest. But when one thinks of some recent artistic creations—such as Max Headroom, the Coca-Cola figure who exists only on the video screen—then Jameson's formula can be seen to have a legitimate specific application (or "local validity" as he might say), the connections between capitalist reification and a particular use of simulacra being especially clear. But when the search for the "logic of the simulacrum" is overgeneralized, it not only leads to oversimplification but also blinds us to those contemporary works of art which challenge such a logic. Jameson is aware of this: "in the most interesting postmodernist works . . . one can detect a more positive conception of relationship [than the censure of fragmentation] which restores its proper tension to the notion of difference itself. This new mode of relationship through difference may sometimes be an achieved new and original way of thinking and perceiving; more often it takes the form of an impossible imperative to achieve that new mutation [in perceptual organs] in what can perhaps no longer be called consciousness" (p. 75). Jameson all too quickly discards the possibility of a positive conception of relationship through difference for the latter negative critique of postmodernism throughout most of his essay.

As we have seen, Jameson implicitly attributes Perelman's schizophrenic aesthetic to the process of reification in late capitalist society. It is interesting, therefore, to find Perelman and others claiming that their aesthetic is based on a critique of precisely that same fragmenting process. When Steve McCaffery writes, for instance, that "Marx's notion of commodity fetishism . . . has been central to my own considerations of reference in language" (*The L=A=N=G=U=A=G=E Book,* 189; hereafter *LB*), we at least have to examine this claim before denouncing the poetry. Such an examination reveals that foregrounding the materiality of language, far from being a schizophrenic disorder or an hallucinatory escapism, is intended instead, according to Bruce Andrews, as "a political writing practice that unveils demystifies the creation & sharing of meaning" (*LB,* 135). Words are never our own, Ron Silliman reminds us. "Rather, they are our own usages of a determinate coding passed down to us like all other products of civilization . . ." (*LB,* 167). The unveiling of this determinate coding and the ways in which that coding reinforces the capitalist power structure lies behind the "schizophrenic" poetry of Perelman, McCaffery, Andrews, Silliman, and others.

Evidently for Jameson the material signifier exemplifies the process of reification in late capitalist society. Even fellow poet Jackson Mac Low asks, "What could be more of a fetish or more alienated than slices of language stripped of reference?" (*L=A=N=G=U=A=G=E* 4: 23). Indeed, if all that these poets were doing was isolating language from its social context, then they would be perpetuating reification. But is that what Perelman and others are doing? A material signifier by itself neither perpetuates nor liberates us from reification. Only how we perceive the social relations inscribed within the signifier will determine its particular political effect.

A close look at "China" (*Primer,* 60–61) will illustrate the aesthetic complexity and political resonance of the poem. The first few lines read as follows:

We live on the third world from the sun. Number three.
Nobody tells us what to do.

The people who taught us how to count were being very
kind.

It's always time to leave.

If it rains, you either have your umbrella or you don't.

The wind blows your hat off.

The sun rises also.

I'd rather the stars didn't describe us to each other; I'd
Rather we do it for ourselves.

The first thing to notice is the role of the title in this poem. The first line, made up of simple sentences, projects a very broad contextual frame for these statements. The first sentence, for example, could be said by anyone on earth familiar with our position in the solar system. The frame can be narrowed slightly by recognizing that such a statement most often is spoken in a classroom or in some other teaching context, but the speaker, whether teacher or pupil, remains obscure. The sentence's proximity to the title, however, greatly reduces its contextual scope, implying some relationship to China, that implication being reinforced by the "third world" pun. The reiteration of third in "Number three" strengthens the classroom association, the phrase being spoken, perhaps, by a Chinese student straightforwardly proclaiming her independence: "Nobody tells us what to do." Living on the only known inhabited planet, our actions are not dictated by some other world. Or as members of a young revolutionary society, the Chinese reject any external pressure, unlike many other third world nations.

The second line seems to lack any apparent connection to the first, its isolation reinforced by the unusual space between the lines. Nevertheless, there are several possible connections between the two. The possible classroom theme of the first line becomes explicit in the second. The ambiguity of tone in the second arises in part from the defiant tone of the first line, leading us to ask whether we should take the second statement at face value, or read it as sarcasm, or both. Such ambiguity fits well with the anticapitalist overtones of the first line: although mathematics is an important practical tool, it can also lead to the reduction of things to some arbitrary quantitative value. And perhaps most ironic is that the people who taught us how to count were telling us what to do, a hint at the problematic relations between missionary work and imperialism in China's recent past (note the past tense).

But how does that lead to "It's always time to leave"? The past tense of line two suggests that those kind of teachers have gone, have been super-seded. Situations change with time. Thus any attempt to stop change, to perpetuate the status quo, will naturally meet with resistance. Line three, then, can be seen as a revolutionary slogan. A second possible meaning to this line arises, however, when it is followed by "If it rains, you either have your umbrella or you don't." If we read line four literally—if we choose not to read it figuratively as an extension of the revolution theme—then line three becomes part of a new mini-narrative, leaving the first one behind and thereby acting out its own axiomatic content. Now someone has left and is outside, exposed to the weather. If "you" has prepared for a shift in events, then she has a better chance of weathering the storm that will blow her hat off in line five. Line six then seems to follow quite naturally if we add a "but" as the first word. But it also returns to the solar theme of the first line, this time reversing the perceptual frame from a heliocentric to a geocentric one (as well as adding a humorous self-conscious literariness in its allusion to Heming-way, whose characters are tossed around by events more often than taking control of them as the Chinese do).

The oppression/self-determination theme reaches a provisional climax in line seven: "I'd rather the stars didn't describe us to each other; I'd rather we do it for ourselves." Besides the astrological allusion, the hint at China's geopolitical positioning between the two stars—the USSR and the USA—returns. The Chinese would rather be a third world. In addition, line seven hints at the position of the reader, left on her own to participate in the construction of the poem's meaning.

As Jameson has suggested, the lines that follow seem much like a docu-mentary montage of various isolated glimpses of Chinese life under the revolution ("The landscape is motorized"), a nation just learning how to talk in the excitement of new uniforms, flags, industry, fireworks, and Utopian dreams.

What is missing from "China" are the standard syntactical conjunctions and explicitly coherent subject matter common to everyday speech. But when have these components been necessary for poetry? At least since Pound's "In a Station of the Metro" parataxis to many has seemed *the* "poetic" form of juxtaposition, with its demand that the reader fill in the gaps between the lines, as we have been doing with "China." Unlike Pound's poem, however, the gaps in "China" are not metaphoric but, as in Stein's *Tender Buttons*, metonymic. The meaning of the poem develops along the axis of contiguity, the sentences establishing an interlocking, sometimes contradictory and polysemous, series of semantic frames which continually qualify and redirect the overall narrative movement. (See chapter five for an elaboration on this syntactical praxis.) The foregrounded structuration of this poem, far from obliterating the meaning of its content, *adds* a formal dimension of meaning quite consistent with the content's insistence on change, perceptual renewal, and self-determination. The structure of the poem itself can be seen as a metaphor for the historical process that Poulantzas describes in his complex, conflictual model of the social formation.

Contrary to the implications of Jameson's schizophrenia analogy, Perelman isn't suggesting that we can do without narration, only that (1) the particular narrations into which we are inserted are coded justifications for the status quo, and (2) there are alternative ways of structuring (constituting) our experiences. Such alternatives *foreground* our social relations, not reify them.

Ironically, Perelman and other so-called Language poets can be seen to meet Jameson's call for a new political art whose "aesthetic of cognitive mapping" in this confusing postmodern space of late capitalism may achieve "a breakthrough to some as yet unimaginable new mode of representing [the world space of multinational capital], in which we may again begin to grasp our positioning as individual and collective subjects and regain a capacity to act and struggle which is at present neutralized by our spatial as well as our social confusion" ("Postmodernism," 92). The foregrounding of the materiality of the signifier at this time is meant to draw attention to the socially inscribed gestural nature of language, the dialectical consciousness of which capitalism seeks to repress by valorizing what Ron Silliman calls the "disappearance of the word/appearance of the world syndrome" of realism. Seen in this context, poems like "China" must be taken as critiques of and Utopian compensation for the reification of language in late capitalism. This critique of reification is the subject of the next chapter. Its compensation is the subject of chapter five.

FOUR

Realism and Reification

The Poetics and Politics of
Three Language Poets

In the "Politics of Poetry" double issue of $L=A=N=G=U=A=G=E$ magazine (9/10 [October 1979] Bruce Andrews and Charles Bernstein published a forum on the views of various so-called Language poets on the politics of their writing. The common editorial procedure for that magazine was to publish related passages from the works of writers from other fields or times. Thus the editors included, without accompanying commentary, a passage from Terry Eagleton's review of *Aesthetics and Politics*, a collection of documents from the famous Brecht-Lukács debate on realism and modernism. Part of Eagleton's passage reads:

> Consider this curious paradox. A Marxism which had for too long relegated signifying practices to the ghostly realms of the superstructure is suddenly confronted by a semiotic theory which stubbornly insists upon the materiality of the signifier. A notion of the signifier as a mere peg of occasion for a signified, a transparent container brimfull with the plenitude of a determinate meaning, is dramatically overturned. On the contrary, the signifier must be grasped as the product of material labour inscribed in a specific apparatus—a moment in that ceaseless work and play of signification whose sheer heterogeneous productivity is always liable to be repressed by the bland self-possession of sign systems. A centuries old metaphysic of the signified is rudely subverted: the signified is no more than that always half-effaced, infinitely deferred effect of signifying practice which glides impudently out of our reach even as we try to close our fist upon it, scurrying back as it endlessly does into the privilege of becoming a signifier itself. . . . The literary names for this are realism and representation. (*New Left Review*, 21–22)

What role does this passage play in the double issue of $L=A=N=G=U=A=G=E$? Andrews and Bernstein most likely have read the rest of Eagleton's essay and know that the passage is a caricature of the French journal *Tel Quel's* position on realism (a position articulated by Philippe Sollers, Julia Kristeva, and other frequent contributors). So to what extent does the above passage characterize, rather than caricature, the view on realism of a few or more Language poets?

53

Certainly the *Tel Quel* position on realism hardly matches the common caricature of the "vulgar" Marxist critic—the party hack who demands that all art provide a "realistic" representation of the evils of capitalism and the progress of the socialist state. But the Marxist background for the positions on realism of certain Language poets begins not with "vulgar" Marxism but with the more sophisticated models argued for by Georg Lukács, members of the Frankfurt School, and Louis Althusser.

Fredric Jameson's recent challenge to the poetic practice of the so-called Language school (see his "Postmodernism, or The Cultural Logic of Late Capitalism") makes urgent the need to formulate the aesthetical-political positions of these poets. Ironically, Jameson and some Language writers all base their critiques of certain literary modes on the notion of reification. But this single notion has led to quite opposing conclusions (see also my "Jameson's Perelman: Reification and the Material Signifier"). The Jameson-Language school debate, so to speak, in many ways resembles the Brecht-Lukács debates earlier in this century. Not surprisingly, Jameson and members of the Language school base their own arguments in part on arguments developed in those earlier debates. For a full understanding of the positions on realism of Ron Silliman, Steve McCaffery, and Bruce Andrews, then, we need to review the crucial issues of the Brecht-Lukács debates, as well as the modification of those issues by Louis Althusser.

Lukács, the Frankfurt School, and Althusser

In the essay "Reification and the Consciousness of the Proletariat" Lukács offers the following definition of reification: "Its basis is that a relation between people takes on the character of a thing and thus acquires a 'phantom objectivity', an autonomy that seems so strictly rational and all-embracing as to conceal every trace of its fundamental nature: the relation between people" (p. 83). The concept is a translation, so to speak, of Marx's notion of commodity-fetishism, which in turn depends on Marx's distinction between use-value and exchange-value. "The utility of a thing," Marx writes, "makes it a use-value. But this utility is not a thing of the air. Being limited by the physical properties of the commodity, it has no existence apart from that commodity" (*Capital,* 1:36). (This concern with the physical properties of the commodity recurs in the Language school's emphasis on the materiality of the signifier.) Exchange-value, on the other hand, exists as an abstraction apart from the commodity, its physical properties no longer in sight. What determines the exchange-value of the commodity is not any quality of the product itself but the quantity of labor time that went into its making; that is, exchange-value is a social relation, a result of the labor process. "A commodity is therefore a curious thing," Marx continues, "simply because in it the social character of men's labour appears to them as an objective character stamped upon the product of that labour: because the relation of the producers to the sum total of their own labour is presented to them as a social relation, existing not between themselves, but between the products of their labour" (p. 72). Just as in religion the creations of the human brain become hypostatized as independent objects (gods, angels, devils), so the products of workers' labor become fetishized.

Lukács then appropriates Max Weber's notion of rationalization (Taylorization, the increasing fragmentation of social processes into discrete quantifiable units) and Hegel's concept of estrangement (the objectification of spirit, the fragmentation of subjectivity into objectivity) into his own conception of reification as a process of fragmentation of the social totality. Through the process of reification human beings are alienated from their true nature as social producers, their own labor itself becoming a commodity, a thing to be sold on the market like any other commodity. Since society for Lukács is an organic expressive totality—a totality in which "the individual elements incorporate [or express] the structure of the whole" (*History*, 198)—then each level (economic, aesthetic, political, etc.) is structurally homologous to the totality's essential level: the mode of production. Consequently, the effects of a mode of production based on commodity-production will influence all other levels. A mode of production, in other words, which gives rise to reification will cause that reification to spread throughout the totality.

Reification is no accident but part of an overall historical process. For Hegel the historical dialectic represented the subject of history's, or Absolute Spirit's, coming to consciousness of itself. Estrangement is not to be mourned but to be seen as a necessary moment of such a coming-to-consciousness, during which the subject of history becomes manifest in the objective world and then recognizes itself in those objects, thus reconciling once and for all the schism between subjectivity and objectivity. Just so, reification for Lukács is the historically determined moment when the subject of history—now the proletariat—becomes wholly objectified. What follows, then, is the proletariat's recognition of itself as history's subject, as the end of the material process of dialectical contradiction. The immediate task of the Marxist is the raising of class consciousness and revolution.

Lukács claims, however, that such consciousness is not inevitable, but only a "concrete possibility"; in other words, historical conditions make such consciousness possible but not automatic. Class consciousness must be fought for by those who have seen through what Lukács calls the "veil of reification." Literature, determined by its isomorphic relationship to commodity production, thus becomes an arena for class struggle. In *Realism In Our Time* Lukács argues that the modernism of Joyce, Musil, and Kafka contributes to the reifying effects of commodity production because such art is "anti-real." The world view implied by these authors takes the appearance of fragmented reality as truth. The individual for these writers, Lukács claims, "is by nature solitary, unable to enter into relationships with other human beings" (p. 20). These authors fail to recognize that such thrownness-into-being, as Heidegger puts it, is only the historically determined state of modern society, not a universal condition of life. The technique of stream-of-consciousness in Joyce's *Ulysses*, for instance, presents life as an aimless, directionless agglomeration of random, static details. In the more realistic work of Thomas Mann, on the other hand, such as *Lotte in Weimar*, every "person or event, emerging momentarily from the stream and vanishing again, is given a specific weight, a definite position, in the pattern of the whole" (*Realism*, 18). Realism (or more accurately "critical realism" as distinguished from "naturalism" and socialist realism) reveals the connections between the individual and the social totality, thereby showing the relationships which have been occluded by reification. Realism thus becomes a tool for consciousness raising, while other literary modes only perpetuate our present mystification.

Not all Marxist aestheticians, however, share Lukács's view of the political effects of realism. The classic counter to Lukács's position, of course, is that of Bertolt Brecht and his associates of the Frankfurt School; among Marxist aesthetic theories, this one has most influenced the Language school. Brecht agrees with Lukács that literature must reveal some truth in order to be effective: "The ruling classes use lies oftener than before—and bigger ones. To tell the truth is clearly an ever more urgent task" (*Aesthetics*, 80). But *how* that truth was told is the issue. "Realism is not a mere question of form," Brecht continues. "Were we to copy the style of these [nineteenth century bourgeois] realists, we would no longer be realists. . . . Reality changes; in order to represent it, modes of representation must change. . . . The oppressors do not work in the same way in every epoch" (p. 82). Realism, in other words, is a historically determined mode of representation that cannot be made into an ahistorical absolute, as Lukács seems to do. If modern reality is indeed determined by commodity production—and Brecht and the Frankfurt School agree that it is—then earlier representative modes are not only outdated but will serve to confirm the "realistic," empiricist notions that the bourgeoisie passes off as natural, as common sense.

"The unity represented by art and the pure humanity of its persons are unreal," Herbert Marcuse wrote; "they are the counter image of what occurs in social reality" ("The Affirmative Character of Culture," 102). Such Utopian visions of unity spur the desire for change. But those desires then "are either internalized as the duty of the individual soul (to achieve what is constantly betrayed in the external existence of the whole) or represented as objects of art (whereby their reality is relegated to a realm essentially different from that of everyday life)" (p. 114). The reification of modern society must be shown, Marcuse suggests, not some ideal realm of the past. Reification may even have its positive role: "In suffering the most extreme reification man triumphs over reification" (p. 116). The Language school's foregrounding of the material signifier attempts such a triumph, offering seemingly meaningless words in order to draw attention to the production of meaning itself.

Such is Brecht's position as a dramatist. Walter Benjamin, in his discussion of Brecht's "Epic Theater" in "The Author as Producer," writes that at "the centre of [Brecht's] experiments stands man. The man of today; a reduced man, therefore, a man kept on ice in a cold world. But since he is the only man we've got, it is in our interests to know him" (*Understanding Brecht*, 100). Benjamin describes Brecht's method as follows:

> . . . Brecht went back to the most fundamental and original elements of theatre. He confined himself, as it were, to a podium, a platform. He renounced plots requiring a great deal of space. Thus he succeeded in altering the functional relationship between stage and audience, text and production, producer and actor. Epic theatre, he declared, must not develop actions but represent conditions. As we shall presently see, it obtains its 'conditions' by allowing the actions to be interrupted. Let me remind you of the 'songs', whose principal function consists in interrupting the action. Here, then—that is to say, with the principle of interruption—the epic theatre adopts a technique which has become familiar to you in recent years through film and radio, photography and the press. I speak of the technique of montage, for montage interrupts the context into which it is inserted. (*Understanding Brecht*, 99)

What is the political effect of these interruptions? First, they work against creating an illusion of life, of audience identification with the characters as people other than actors on a stage. Just as the Russian Futurists "laid bare the device" in order to draw attention to the medium itself, Brecht foregrounds the dramatic medium in order to "estrange" the audience from its usual expectation. Second, "It [interruption] brings the action to a standstill in mid-course," Benjamin explains, "and thereby compels the spectator to take up a position towards the action, and the actor to take up a position towards his part" (p. 100). The spectators and actors are forced into active positions rather than the traditional passive ones of bourgeois mimetic art, in which the "realistic" technique carries the spectators and actors along on a predetermined path. And third, in an increasingly totalitarian society— reification having spread throughout the totality, German Fascism having come to power, Stalinist oppression having obliterated free thought—such a demand for active, critical thought works against the "naturalness" of the status quo.

Falling back on traditional modes of representation, then, will force no one to think about how such mimetic illusions come about and, by extension, how ideological justifications come about. Realism, even in the hands of the committed Communist artist, Benjamin claims, "functions in a counter-revolutionary way so long as the writer experiences his solidarity with the proletariat only *in the mind* and not as a producer" (p. 91). Like any other progressive producer, authors must pursue the "functional transformation," as Brecht put it, of the artistic means of production—which have been appropriated from their bourgeois context—liberating those means from the regressive uses to which they are put under capitalism.

How far the Frankfurt School has come from Lukács's position is clearest in the theoretical works of Theodor Adorno. Ironically, Adorno's interest in Marxism began with his reading of Lukács's *History and Class Consciousness.* (See Susan Buck-Morss's study, *The Origin of Negative Dialectics,* and Martin Jay's *The Dialectical Imagination* for a discussion of Adorno's relationship to Lukács.) For Lukács the antinomies of bourgeois thought, such as Kant's dualism of phenomenon and noumenon, grew out of the increasingly reified conditions of capitalist society. Lukács's resolution of these antinomies, by Hegelianizing Kant, resulted in Lukács's belief that the proletariat was the class which could finally resolve Kant's epistemological dilemma. But for Adorno there is no positive *Aufhebung* of the dialectic between these antinomies, as Fredric Jameson explains:

> [T]he very mark of the modern experience of the world itself is that precisely such [a resolution] is impossible, and that the primacy of the subject is an illusion, that subject and outside world can never find such ultimate identity or atonement under present historical circumstances. Yet if that ultimate synthesis toward which dialectical thought moves turns out to be unattainable it must not be thought that either of the terms of that synthesis, either of the conceptual opposites which are its subject and object, are any more satisfactory in their own right. (*Marxism and Form,* 55–56)

If bourgeois Marxist theorists have no direct access to the *Ding-an-sich,* in other words, they nevertheless are in the best position to criticize society precisely because of the process of reification. "Only when the established order has become the measure of all things," writes Adorno, "does its mere reproduction in the realm of consciousness become truth" (*Prisms,* 26). When commodity production affects all levels of society, that is, then the "truth" of that society is reification itself. Only in the complete separation of mental and physical production, Adorno claims, can cultural production be completely free to criticize all of society, "the truth of which consists in bringing untruth to consciousness of itself" (p. 28). Such truth is disruptive in that dialectical thought can never rest on a positive note but must continue to search out the positive and negative sides to all social phenomena. As such, though the product of reification, dialectics "means intransigence towards all reification" (p. 31). The relationship of Adorno's negative dialectics to art comes in the view that the "successful work . . . is not one which resolves objective contradictions in a spurious harmony, but one which expresses the idea of harmony negatively by embodying the contradictions, pure and un- compromised, in its innermost structure" (p. 32). In a curious way the totality, so prized by Lukács, has been turned inside-out, reification now being total. There can be no comfort in such knowledge, however: "Cultural criticism finds itself faced with the final stage of the dialectic of culture and barbarism. To write poetry after Auschwitz is barbaric" (p. 34).

Adorno's negative dialectics, in its denial of Hegel's positive synthesizing movement, comes close to the structuralist (or poststructuralist) positions of Derrida and Althusser, who in quite different ways appropriate Saussurean concepts into their own ideology critiques. Such a move, as much as the Frankfurt School's Critical Theory, lies behind the political claims of some Language poets, especially Silliman's (as we shall see). While the application of the linguistic model or metaphor carries with it the danger of allegorism or homology—the reduction of one field of study into the categories of another—such a move may be justified, as Jameson points out, by pointing to "the concrete character of the social life of the so-called advanced countries today, which offer the spectacle of a world from which nature as such has been eliminated, a world saturated with messages and information, whose intricate commodity network may be seen as the very prototype of a system of signs" (*Prison-House*, ix).

Saussure's first theoretical move in attempting to outline a method for analyzing sign systems was his distinction between synchronic and diachronic, a move that would return in different form in Althusser's distinction between structural and expressive totality. In order to counter the geneticist fallacy of semantics, Saussure insisted that for the speaker the language as a total system is complete at every moment; only the current meaning of a word matters. Therefore, the Historical linguists, in their dependence on etymology and other evolutionary (or diachronic) models, could not sufficiently explain the total structure of a language at a given moment. They could explain individual, isolated changes of a word, but they could not explain the immediate (or synchronic), lived experience of meaning itself. While Saussure's emphasis on the ahistorical, static, synchronic conception of language seems at first at odds with Marxism's emphasis on history, that concept surprisingly leads to a perception of the social construction of language quite compatible with Marx's emphasis on the social construction of value.

The power of Saussure's insight lies in his shift from a substantialist concept of meaning to a relational one. Words are no longer to be seen as acquiring meaning through their relation to the things they name but to all the other words of the sign system. Any sign, Saussure claims, is made up of two sides: the signifier (the vocal sounds of the word) and the signified (the concept to which the signifier refers). A sign's meaning is arbitrary in that its signifier has no essential connection to its signified; "cat," "chat," and "gato" all refer to the same concept. The sign acquires its meaning through its negative relationship to all other signs of the system; that is, "cat" refers to the concept of the animal because we distinguish it from "cad" and "mat." "All of which simply means," Saussure tells us, "that *in language there are only differences*. More than that: a difference normally presupposes some positive terms between which it is established; but in language there are only differences *without positive terms*" (cited in Jameson, *Prison-House*, 15). Meaning results from the social contract, so to speak, that establishes the perceived differences between "cat," "cad," "dog," and so on. Any claim to a natural connection between a word and a concept, then, misperceives the social nature of meaning. Just so, for Marxist critics any claim to a natural value, natural right, or natural hierarchy misperceives the social construction of value, rights, and social orders.

Saussure's next move is to distinguish *langue* from *parole*. *Langue* refers to the total synchronic system of signs through which a specific *parole*, or act of speech, makes sense. *Langue* is the total ensemble of speech conventions which makes any *parole* possible. But the *langue* has no existence in itself; it only comes into being through the act of *parole*. Through these concepts Saussure provides a way of thinking about the relationship between parts and wholes without separating and subordinating one to the other, as the New Grammarians did with categories of species, genus, and so on. The totality structures the possibilities of its specific manifestations, but it exists only in them; as Althusser puts it, the totality is immanent in its effects through a metonymic relation of causality. This conception of the totality and the part avoids the substantialist traps of organicist notions of totality, such as the notion of a collective unconscious; at the same time it avoids the positivist claims that all there are are parts, the whole seen as an idealist projection.

So where does realism come in? First, Saussure's conception of meaning as an effect of a system of differential relations, as we have seen, calls into question any claim to a natural connection between language and the real. I would claim that all realisms, in one way or another, posit such a natural relationship, and thus are to be seen as ideological projections. Such a situation must today be seen as negative, for reasons soon to be clarified. But "realism" as a particular aesthetic mode in the early nineteenth century was a revolutionary force. Jameson describes the revolutionary role that bourgeois realism once played:

> that processing operation variously called narrative mimesis or realistic represen-
> tation has as its historic function the systematic undermining and demystification,
> the secular "decoding," of those preexisting inherited traditional or sacred nar-
> rative paradigms which are its initial givens. In this sense, the novel plays a
> significant role in what can be called a properly bourgeois cultural revolution—
> that immense process of transformation whereby populations whose life habits
> were formed by other, now archaic, modes of production are effectively pro-
> grammed for life and work in the new world of market capitalism. The "objective"
> function of the novel is thereby implied: to its subjective and critical, analytic,
> corrosive mission must now be added the task of producing as though for the first
> time that very life world, that very "referent"—the newly quantifiable space of
> extension and market equivalence, the new rhythms of measurable time, the new
> secular and "disenchanted" object world of the commodity system, with its post-
> traditional daily life and its bewilderingly empirical, "meaningless," and con-
> tingent *Umwelt*—of which this new narrative discourse will then claim to be the
> "realistic" reflection. (*Political Unconscious,* 152)

In order for these processes of demystification and of the constitution of a new, properly capitalist, "referent" to come into play, however, there must be an equally revolutionary change in the concept of the subject, the creation of the monadic cogito, the subject. The "free agent" of capitalism must be fashioned out of the more decentered effect of subjectivity in precapitalist society. While the monadic subject is in one sense a mirage, it is nevertheless "in some fashion an objective reality. For the lived experience of individual consciousness as a monadic and autonomous center of activity is not some mere conceptual error, which can be dispelled by the taking of thought and by scientific rectification: it has a quasi-institutional status, performs ideological functions, and is susceptible to historical causation and produced and reinforced by other objective instances, determinants, and mechanisms" (p. 153).

Jameson's notion of the constitution of the subject draws on the Althusserian translation of Lacan into a Marxist theory of ideology. Lacan, having translated psychoanalysis into Saussurean linguistics, sees the creation of the subject as an effect of the process of signification. Through a series of alienations or separations the infant proceeds from a state of undifferentiated existence—in which neither subject nor object can be distinguished, the only distinctions being between total satiety and void—to a position of predication. But predication is only possible once the infant has been inserted into the Symbolic Order, the *langue* or potential for signification, in which both subject and object have been projected or alienated into the position of signifiers. The subject-as-signifier implies the positing of the self as other, the splitting of the self and the insertion into the radical alterity of the signifying chain. Language, that social nexus of relationships existing before our birth, speaks us, so to speak, before we speak it. Herein lies the key to a Marxist recuperation of Lacan's psychoanalysis.

Althusser, in a move quite influential on various Language poets, translates the Symbolic Order into ideology, seeing it as the condition of possibility of the subject's praxis within society. Ideology, like language, exists before us and mediates between us and the real—that absent register that shows itself only in its effects, its frustrations of the fulfillment of desire, of reunification of subject and object. Or as Althusser puts it: "Ideology represents the imaginary relationship of individuals to their real conditions of existence" (*Lenin and Philosophy*, 162). No society, therefore, can do without ideology for no society can ever come into direct contact with the real, the real being History, that absent cause which determines the effects of the totality but exists nowhere outside of those effects. Such a position could be seen as Adorno without Hegel, Hegel's expressive totality having been replaced by Saussure's diacritical *langue*. If no society can do without ideology, then again any claim to a natural or true relation to the real is "ideological," unaware of its own socially mediated (i.e. not immediate) awareness. Any claim to realism, then, will in this sense be ideological.

Language and Reification

Of all the so-called Language poets Ron Silliman has carried on the most sustained analysis of the interplay of realism and reification. Drawing on the theory of the Russian Formalists (particularly Roman Jakobson), the Frankfurt School (particularly Walter Benjamin), Roland Barthes, Jacques Derrida, and most importantly Louis Althusser, Silliman's poetic theory and practice explore the likelihood that capitalism has "a specific 'reality' which is passed through the language and thereby imposed on its speakers" (*The L=A=N=G=U=A=G=E Book*, 123; hereafter *LB*). Althusser and Poulant-zas's notions of social formation and overdetermination complicate any dis-cussion of a "single, capitalist, world economy," as Silliman has stated (*LB*, 167)—a problem he inherits from the Frankfurt School's reliance on the Hegelian expressive totality. But Silliman's generalizations about capitalism and reification can be seen to have a local validity, as Jameson has put it, in that the sustaining power of capitalism has been the increasing "impression" or "existential experience" of capitalism as a thoroughly totalizing, seemingly inescapable system (see Marcuse's *One-Dimensional Man*) or a seemingly natural and inevitable state of affairs (as the promoters of capitalism would have us believe). In the Age of Reagan, capitalism's reach certainly appears total, extending to religion, education, and the sense of self (witness such strategic events as the 1984 Olympics and the 1987 Miss USA Pageant, in which individual achievement is transformed into a victory for U.S. capital-ism). When the total population is trained to equate the word "freedom" solely with "capitalism" and "America," then the power of language as ideological mediation becomes especially clear.

But Silliman's notion of a single capitalist system also can be valid so long as one keeps in mind that capitalism, though not a pure and single entity, is nevertheless the hegemonic influence, the structure-in-dominance, of West-ern society. For if capitalism's effects were total, then there would be no possibility for people such as Silliman to escape its influence, in however partial a way. Silliman acknowledges this by pointing out that, although the role of ideology is to repress any notions or impulses that may conflict with the smooth operation of the hegemonic structure, repression "does not, fortunately, abolish the existence of the repressed element which continues as a contradiction, often visible, in the social fact. As such, it continues to wage the class struggle of consciousness" (*LB*, 126).

Silliman's equation of realism and reification depends on what he sees as the essential differences between tribal society and modern capitalist society due to the historical development of language. If the mode of production of a given society determines the language of that society, then the stage of historical development, Silliman claims, "determines the *natural* laws (or, if you prefer the terminology, the underlying structures) of poetry" (*LB*, 122).

And if that language determines the consciousness of the members of that society, then poetry, as a language practice, plays a role in ideological production and is an indicator of the social assumptions about language. How *extensive* a role poetry plays in ideological production and how *thoroughly* the language habits of a given society are determined by its mode of production, however, is not clear in Silliman's formulation. Nevertheless, whatever the ultimate validity of such a formulation, Silliman's contrast of the language habits of tribal society (which functions as an ideal and Utopian projection of his politics) to modern capitalist society does reveal, in my view, the subtle relationships between linguistic and ideological production. The tribe, Silliman claims, is structured as a "group," a social organization which integrates individuals and provides a backdrop against which individual differences can be perceived (as opposed to the "series" of capitalist society, in which individuals are reduced to mere ciphers in an equation). In tribal society, reference exists in its "primary form":

> In its primary form, reference takes on the character of a gesture and an object, such as the picking up of a stone to be used as a tool. Both gesture and object carry their own integrities and are not confused: a sequence of gestures is distinct from the objects which may be involved, as distinct as the labor process is from its resultant commodities. A sequence of gestures forms a discourse, not a description. It is precisely the expressive integrity of the gestural nature of language which constitutes the meaning of the "nonsense" syllables in tribal poetries; its persistence in such characteristics of Skelton's poetry as his rhyme is that of the trace. (*LB*, 125)

The difference between "the gestural nature of language" and "the nature of gestural language" reveals much in Silliman's conception of the inherent social nature of language. "Gesture," the manipulation of objects (words) in the creation of language, is not simply one historically specific condition of a particular society's language habits but the *nature* of language in general. The gestural makes its appearance in the conspicuous materiality of the elements of language organization, such as sound, rhyme, and rhythm. In the conventional organization of material elements in the sonnet, for example, one can see the traces of the social production of language. One never loses sight of the gesture behind the object; in Saussurean terms, one never loses sight of the signifier behind the signified; in Marxist terms, one never loses sight of the labor process behind the commodity. However, according to Silliman:

> What happens when a language moves toward and passes into a capitalist stage of development is an anaesthetic transformation of the perceived tangibility of the word, with corresponding increases in its descriptive and narrative capacities, preconditions for the invention of "realism," the optical illusion of reality in capitalist thought. These developments are tied directly to the nature of reference in language, which under capitalism is transformed (deformed) into referentiality. (*LB*, 125)

However useful the distinction between reference and referentiality may be, the important point here is the process of the increasing transparency of the signifier. The word which no longer reveals the gesture behind it is, therefore, the reified word. Lukács's definition of reification can now be read as follows: "Its basis is that a relation between people [language] takes on the character of a thing [the transparent, self-sufficient word] and thus acquires a 'phantom objectivity', an autonomy that seems so strictly rational and all-embracing as to conceal every trace [gesture] of its fundamental nature: the relation between people."

It is instructive to compare Silliman's concept of the gestural with Walter Benjamin's concept of aura. In "The Work of Art in the Age of Mechanical Reproduction" Benjamin distinguishes between the original art object and its reproduction. The original is marked by four qualities or conditions: (1) its unique existence; (2) its relative permanence; (3) its cultic use value; and (4) its unapproachability. The reproduction, on the other hand, exhibits the opposite conditions: (1) its reproducibility; (2) its transitory existence; (3) its commodified exchange value; and (4) its relative immediacy. A further distinction related to the third and fourth conditions above is between the mode of participation or reception of each. The relationship between the viewer and the original object constitutes what Benjamin refers to as the work's aura, its essential and discrete otherness, its distance from the perceiver. "The definition of aura as a 'unique phenomenon of a distance however close it may be'," Benjamin explains, "represents nothing but the formulation of the cult value of the work of art in categories of space and time perception. . . . The essentially distant object is the unapproachable one" (*Illuminations*, 243, n.5). With the increasing reification of modern life, however, and its concomitant demand for realism, visual art is stripped of its aura by means of photographic reproduction.

It is important to note here that the work's aura is not an ontological constituent of the work itself but instead a result of a social context (the cultic object situated in a cathedral viewed by awed and reverent worshippers). This is important because Benjamin's complaint is not so much against reproductions themselves (although this does seem to play a role here) but against the *age* that demands such re-presentations: the imperial age of capitalism. In fact, mechanical reproduction even in the present age, Benjamin claims, has its positive side: "The progressive reaction [of the masses to film] is characterized by the direct, intimate fusion of visual and emotional enjoyment with the orientation of the expert" (*Illuminations*, 234). (For an elaboration of a similar point, see his "What is Epic Theater?" in *Illuminations*, 147–54.)

Two questions remain, however, in extending Benjamin's "aura" to Silliman's "gesturality": first, what is the literary equivalent to the original painting? In other words, can there be an original locus of the poem? Peter Bürger argues that "in literature, there is no technical innovation that could have produced an effect comparable to that of photography in the fine arts" (*Theory of the Avant-Garde,* 32). The effect he refers to is photography's appropriation of painting's mimetic role; how could a painting compete with the photograph's reproduction of reality? As a result, or so it seems, the pictorial arts were forced to develop in a non-mimetic direction, towards abstraction. And the second question is, can there be a mode of mechanical *literary* production which would appropriate some prior mode of literature? Silliman's concept of gesturality provides a possible approach to these questions.

Silliman opens his essay, "Benjamin Obscura," by noting that "Benjamin's characterization of the photograph . . . functions also to note the role of the camera in a crucial step toward the fetishized realism which embodies the capitalist mode of thought. . . . [T]he hand in the process of pictorial reproduction is stripped of its gestural content" (*LB,* 63). By the latter statement Silliman evidently means that the mark of the artist, such as the textured brush stroke or the variation in performance, is effaced from the photograph. At any rate, the translation of aura into gesturality resituates the problematic. We are now not so much concerned with an original object as we are with the entire social matrix out of which all aesthetic objects evolve, the traces of which we see in the gestural dimension of the work. The rise of literary realism thus parallels the rise of photography in the effacement of the gesture. Second, Silliman identifies the development of a mode of mechanical reproduction, the printing press, which transforms an earlier literary mode. "Gutenberg's moveable type erased gesturality from the graphemic dimension of books" (*LB,* 63). The invention of the alphabet, the development of bards, the arrival of the book, and the standardization of spelling, capitalization, etc., also led to the repression of the gesture through the increasing division of literary labor.

But what does all this mean for contemporary poetic practice? First of all, it leads Silliman to explore the ways in which units of meaning integrate into larger units—words into phrases, phrases into sentences, sentences into paragraphs, paragraphs into the total work. What Silliman claims to discover is that the sentence is the hinge between fragments and wholes, the privileged point of focus for his study of reification and language. Use value, as we have seen, depends on the material of the object itself, whereas exchange value ignores that material in order to pass on to something beyond the object (the apotheosis of this being money). By analogy, the use value of a linguistic object involves a concentration on the materiality of that object, while exchange value in language involves passing through the language to something else—meaning. The sentence is the smallest written unit, Silliman claims, which leads to a complete statement (exchange value), yet the sentence in isolation tends to be the largest unit which can be viewed as a material object (use value), keeping the reader's attention focused "at least partly in the present, consuming the text" ("The New Sentence," 205). At this point three possible artistic modes become available: focusing (1) below the sentence, (2) on the sentence, or (3) above the sentence. Realism, in its reach for reference, relies on syllogism, "the classic mode of above-sentence integra-tion" (p. 204) which erases the material dimension of language. *Zaum,* with its dependence on sub-sentence, even sub-word, units, goes in the opposite direction and erases meaning itself. Adorno, in a letter to Benjamin about the latter's "The Work of Art in the Age of Mechanical Reproduction," comments on these two modes:

> The reification of a great work of art is not just loss, any more than the reification of the cinema is all loss. It would be bourgeois reaction to negate the reification of cinema in the name of the ego, and it would border on anarchism to revoke reification of a great work of art in the spirit of immediate use-values. . . . Both bear the stigmata of capitalism, both contain elements of change. . . . Both are torn halves of an integral freedom, to which however they do not add up. (*Aesthetics,* 123).

The dialectical approach to both realism and *zaum,* then, would be a focus on the mediation of the two at a point of their intersection and an insistence on the historical validity and regressiveness of both. Both must be thought at once—and that is what Silliman attempts to do through his focus on the New Sentence, which as we have seen involves the de- and re-contextualization of sentences in order to foreground the logical leap between sentence and syllogism, a leap whose "logic" will be determined by the reader's ideological frame of reference. (Silliman later calls this leap the Parsimony Principle: "Whenever it is possible to integrate two separate elements into a single larger element by imagining them as sharing a common participant, the mind will do so" ["Migratory Meaning," 39].) It is this analysis that lies behind Silli-man's poetic practice, such as the following excerpt from section VII of his poem "Carbon" in *ABC:*

> We, the mind, rainstorm, five card stud, settle, setting doves adrift in the air above the volley. But pigeon's mode's debris, deuce. Atari tacked to cauliflower starts to walk. Jacks scuff along the surface of the plaza, face up. Bulldog in a derby closes the lone eye with a doubloon. Tint the world, fore of clubs, amber of bourbon. Therefore tree's bad as its bark.

Though the passage above, for instance, might appear to be a random collec-tion of words, the reader very likely will begin to recognize or create larger contexts for those words. One should notice, for example, the number of words which refer to card games. Through this process the reader becomes the producer of context rather than the passive recipient. Instead of a trans-parent route to meaning, the reader is faced with the poet's "gesture" of presenting seemingly random words as a poem, their arrangement as well as their content to be read and thought about.

Language poet Steve McCaffery takes a quite different approach to poetic practice, however, even though he too relies heavily on the realism-equals-reification argument. His own position resembles the "anarchist" position that Adorno mentions above, a position associated today with *Tel Quel* semiotics. McCaffery claims that "Marx's notion of commodity fetishism . . . has been central to my own considerations of reference in language—of, in fact, a referentially based language, in general—and to certain 'fetishistic' notions of the relationship of audience and performer. Reference in language is a strategy of promise and postponement; it's the thing that language never is, never can be, but to which language is always moving" (*LB,* 189).

In part, Derrida's notion of *différance*—that meaning is always based on difference (as in Saussure) and on deferral, the presence of the signified always lagging behind or skipping ahead of the signifier—lies behind the "promise and postponement" of McCaffery's conception of language. But McCaffery's notion is more linguistically radical than Derrida's, for McCaffery imagines a point at which one can transcend meaning and achieve a pure presence of the material signifier, a pure use-value or—to the extent that "use-value" carries with it instrumentalist connotations—a pre–use-value. His goal rather is to "step outside of use . . . to see what a hammer is when not in function" ("Death of the Subject"). McCaffery translates the deferring structure of signification into the economic process of exchange as follows:

> Reference in language is a strategy of promise and postponement; it's the thing that language never is, never can be, but to which language is always moving. This linguistic promise that the signified gives of something beyond language I've come to feel as being central to capitalism (the fetish of the commodity) and derived from an earlier theologico-linguistic confidence trick of "the other life." It's this sense of absence as a postponed presence which seems to be the core of narrative (the paradigm art form of the capitalist system) and basic to the word as we use the word in any representational context. (*LB,* 189)

If meaning is like capital, then realism is like capitalism. Having drawn this analogy, McCaffery chooses to subvert capitalism by subverting meaning, by writing a poetry of pure presence not compromised by signification. In order to do so, he writes a poetry that obliterates the referent, presenting the signifier as a cipher: "Cipherality belongs to a synchronic poetics; it is tense-less and free from both reference and alternity, thereby centered within its textual self and available as a primary empirical experience. The cipheral text involves a replacement in readerly function from a reading of words to an experiencing of graphemes, for conventional reading involves the use of referential vectors and it is such vectors that are here removed" ("Death of the Subject". Hence:

```
          al (t        ch
   ph     ysto               kl
                      ee
        apl
      sta
            )
            ry
```

(from "Death of the Subject")

There are two approaches, McCaffery writes, that a reader can take to such a poem: one can treat it as a structural density, a complete object, and de-cipher it; or one can see it as a fragment and en-cipher, or complete, it. In either case, the point is to see the cipher "or emptied sign as a frozen dialectic within a semiotic process, less an active sign than a sign removed from function (and hence deconstructed) to be observed as event per se." Such a conception of reading gives us access to poems such as the following excerpt from Peter Inman's *Ocker:*

> glay qew , (too bone-leave,) lilm than in , quimce,
> book's hollow fix , rning , mim)le always , (other
>   neck meres , ccoon , xamois
>
> mene)dennes) sit)doption.

If we *en*cipher the word "quimce," for example, we will treat it as a complete object and focus on its shape, sound, the internal relationships among letters, its position in space on the page, and so on. If we *de*cipher it, on the other hand, we will try to read it as a fragmentary unit of a larger utterance which is at least partially obscured, or read it as a relative of the word "quince."

McCaffery's own approach to the work of art in the age of mechanical reproduction would very likely also lead to Adorno's charge of anarchism. Just as Benjamin stressed too heavily, in Adorno's view, the progressive nature of film, so McCaffery might be seen to stress too heavily the liberating effects of the tape recorder for the sound poet—the poet who focuses on the material qualities of the aural sign. His optimism grows out of his adoption of Gilles Deleuze and Felix Gauttari's emphasis on desire production (see their *Anti-Oedipus*) and Julia Kristeva's notion of the role of desire in textual production, as can be seen in the following claim: "Sound poetry is much more than simply returning language to its own matter; it is an agency for desire production, for releasing energy flow, for securing the passage of libido in a multiplicity of flows out of the Logos" ("Sound Poetry," *LB*, 88). Sound poetry is contrasted to language, "through its nature as representation, . . . [which] becomes a huge mechanism for suppressing libidinal flow."

McCaffery's concern with language and libidinal flow grows out of his readings in poststructuralist theory, such as Kristeva's distinction between "genotext" and "phenotext." In order to understand Kristeva's distinction, one first must grasp her distinction between what she calls the semiotic (as a noun, not an adjective) and the symbolic (her translation of Lacan's imaginary and symbolic). The semiotic, as Kristeva explains in *Revolution in Poetic Language*, "includes drives, their disposition, and their division of the body, plus the ecological and social system surrounding the body, such as objects and pre-Oedipal relations with parents. The [symbolic] encompasses the emergence of object and subject, and the constitution of nuclei of meaning involving categories: semantic and categorial fields" (p. 86). The semiotic, in other words, continuously resists the organizing structure of the symbolic (the logical and orderly framing of language). Kristeva implicitly charges that the symbolic, because it represses the free play of the drives, is totalitarian. Freeing the drives from such order, then, is an act of liberation.

In the genotext the effects of the semiotic—the prelinguistic articulation of the drives—gain the upper hand over the effects of the linguistic organization through the symbolic, an organization resulting from the repression of unmediated libidinal expression. In the phenotext, as one might guess, the symbolic dominates. But such a distinction never exists in a pure form, Kristeva insists. Rather each text reveals the inseparable dependence and antagonism between the semiotic and the symbolic; the particular dominance of one over the other determines whether a text is genotext or phenotext. The former is marked by the dominance of the play of the phonemic and melodic properties of language at the expense of the representational and communicative goals of language use, while the latter is obviously marked by the opposite. Hence McCaffery's claim that sound poetry is a "gift back to the body of those energy zones repressed, and channelled as charter in the overcoded structure of grammar. To release by a de-inscription those trapped forces of libido" (*LB*, 89).

Whereas Silliman saw the tape recorder as a contributor to alienation (*LB*, 63) because of its obliteration of the gestural, for McCaffery it becomes the tool for creating genotexts never before imaginable. Prior to the 1950s sound poetry remained confined within the limits of the human voice, the most extreme manifestations possible being grunts, howls, and shrieks, as in the work of François Dufrene. But as *zaum* reveals, sounds remained trapped within a teleology of meaning, appearing simply as meaning-fragments rather than as things in themselves. Meaning, as Khlebnikov claimed, was rescued by estrangement, rendering (McCaffery adds) "semantic meaning transcendental, as the destination arrived at by the disautomatization of sound perception" (*LB*, 90). McCaffery continues:

> The body is no longer the ultimate parameter, and voice becomes a point of departure rather than the point of arrival. Realizing also that the tape recorder provides the possibility of a secondary orality predicated upon a graphism (tape, in fact, is but another system of writing where writing is described as any semiotic system of storage) then we can appreciate other immediate advantages: tape liberates composition from the athletic sequentiality of the human body, pieces may be edited, cutting, in effect, becomes the potential compositional basis in which segments can be arranged and rearranged outside of real time performance. . . . Both time and space are harnessed to become less the controlling and more the manipulable factors of audiophony. (*LB*, 90)

The arrival of the tape recorder thus provided a way out of this limitation of the human body.

It is interesting to remember at this point Marx's view of capital, as distinct from capitalism. Communism for him meant not an elimination of capital but an elimination of the mode of production which expropriated capital (surplus labor) from the producers of that surplus (the workers). If ever humanity is to wrest a realm of freedom from the realm of necessity, it needs to build on the productive capabilities made possible by capitalism. Such is the insight of Marx's dialectical thought, which insists on the recognition of the progressive in even the most apparently regressive phenomenon. In contrast to McCaffery's attempt to transgress the limits of meaning—more akin to Jean Baudrillard than to Marx (see the former's *The Mirror of Production*)—it seems more to the point of a Marxist critique of language assumptions in capitalist society to point out the uses to which meaning is put. A better question might be: What is the *meaning* of our particular uses and conceptions of meaning at our particular historical conjuncture? To whose benefit is the present definition of meaning put? The initial insight of semiotics, after all, is that we function not in any immediate way but through the production of sign systems. McCaffery's search here for an immediate relationship to the signifier must be questioned as thoroughly as any other pretense to immediacy. This questioning should extend, furthermore, to his appropriation of the Kristevan conception of the "revolution in poetic language" effected by Mallarmé, Lautreamont, and Joyce, through which they supposedly brought language closer to the semiotic chora, thereby making poetic language "an agency for desire production, for releasing energy flow, for securing the passage of libido in a multiplicity of flows out of the Logos" (McCaffery, *LB*, 88). While claims for the liberating potential of this poetry can and must be made, the claim cannot rest unqualifiedly on the supposed refusal of these poets to impose repressive form on such energy flows. The apparent disorder of *Finnegans Wake* or *Ulysses*, for instance, results from a tightly controlled method of organization. Furthermore, as the Frankfurt School studies of Fascism suggest, libidinal flow does not always produce desirable results. Again, since libidinal flow is always coded through a particular structuring of signification, as Kristeva's concept of the thetic suggests, the question should be who benefits from the present economy of libidinal expression (see Jameson's *Fables of Aggression*).

Recently McCaffery actually has come closer to asking these questions himself, having reached a perhaps more sober assessment of the political potentials of tape. In "And Who Remembers Bobby Sands" he examines the influence of the media as "our culture's dominant mode and posture of telling" (*North of Intention*, 39). Whereas the "Realist" mode of representation was the cultural dominant of an earlier stage of capitalism, this is no longer the case. "The dominant manifestation of narrative is now the media," McCaffery claims, "whose electronic circuitries have imposed a violent shift in cognitive and disseminative modes. Whereas the novel tended to operate under the notions of structure, closure, and an ultimate (albeit often problematized) unity, the narrative of media is characterized by a differential implosion and a structurelessness" (*North of Intention*, 40). Curiously, we are not far from Jameson's own characterization of the cultural dominant in his essay, "Postmodernism, or the Cultural Logic of Late Capitalism." Through quite different methods Jameson and McCaffery arrive at strikingly similar conclusions.

McCaffery explains that the passage from realism to "hyperrealism," or what Jameson calls the simulacrum, is marked by the following shifts in narrative mode: Realist narrative, according to McCaffery, implied a public capable of reciprocal response within the communication network; hyperrealism (narrative with no referent beyond itself), on the other hand, implies a paralyzed audience never given the chance or the inclination to respond to the one-way transmissions of postmodern media such as television.

Whereas such an assessment leads Jameson to an ambivalent, though predominantly negative, view of the possibilities for art in the present environment, it leads McCaffery to an equally ambivalent though positive view:

> The media's narrative economy . . . implodes [all] terms, decommissioning the exchangist nature of transmission economy and rather than providing an alternative structural model is a model that ends structure. Which might lead us to speculate that media narrative, despite its "counter-revolutionary" inertia, has achieved what the molecular recoding strategies of the avant garde have struggled toward through its cumulative litany of failures: the structural abolition of ideological relation, the avoidance of the fetish of value and the disappearance of speaker-listener as structurally determined, ideologically alienated terms. (*North of Intention*, 41)

In other words, following Baudrillard, McCaffery sees the masses' inertia not as their subjugation but as their release from repressive structure. In a cryptic final note he posits "the media's proximity to what Bataille terms 'general economy' that is precisely an economy of waste and irrecoverable expenditure." This economy of waste is contrasted to the repressive organization of narrative structure in an earlier stage of capitalism that allowed for no loose ends—everything was made to fit into an equation. But the postmodern media, McCaffery claims, offer the possibility that " 'fascination' (the narrative condition of the masses) is of an imaginary and not symbolic order, [which might] then [mean that] the revolutionary return of the mother as the techno-phallic goddess will require a certain discourse of its own" (p. 43).

No doubt. But whose interests are inscribed in that discourse? McCaffery's position depends on and could be seen to perpetuate the very orders he loathes. His fellow Language poet James Sherry has written, "The modernists perceived chaos; they did not aspire to it. . . . Everything is already destroyed around us. Yet what can we do to rebuild when the old forms are radioactive with the half-lives that constructed them?" ("Limits of Grammar," 111–12). Bruce Andrews suggests an alternative to both co-optation and flight: " 'wordness', 'eventism'—a way of *reconstituting* language by unpacking the tool box" (*LB*, 33).

In "Writing Social Work & Political Practice" Andrews distinguishes between three possible modes of writing, each mode carrying with it an implied approach to political and epistemological practice. The first mode is realism, which Andrews critiques in much the same way as Silliman and McCaffery do for its "assumptions of reference, representation, transparency, clarity, description, reproduction, positivism" (*LB*, 133). As such, realism relies on a linguistic fetishism. Any political practice growing out of this mode will be either reductionist (socialist realism) or ornamental, complacently reinforcing the status quo by reproducing its basic assumptions of reference. The second mode, "an alternative structuralist mode," characterizes the practice of poets such as McCaffery. This mode focuses on the diacritical structure of the sign. A radical version of this mode would be a poetics of subversion: "an anti-systemic detonation of settled relations, an anarchic liberation of energy flows. Such flows, like libidinal discharges, are thought to exist underneath & independent from the system of language. That system, an armoring, entraps them in codes & grammar" (*LB*, 134). The goal of this poetics, then, is to create a deliberate opacity and dissemination of meaning. Such a poetics abdicates the central struggle over meaning, however, thereby leaving the organization of signs and society to someone or something else:

> The Blob-like social force of interchangeability & *equivalence* (unleashed by the capitalist machine, and so necessary to the commodification of language) precedes us: it has carried quite far the erosion of the system of differences on which signification depends. It's reached the point where a coercive organization of grammar, rhetoric, technical format & ideological symbols is normally imposed in everyday life to even get these eroded differences to do their job any more (an assembly line to deliver meaning, of certain kinds). So to call for a heightening of these deterritorializing tendencies may risk a more homogenized meaninglessness (& one requiring even more coercive props)—an "easy rider" on the flood tide of Capital. (Andrews, *LB*, 135)

Andrews agrees here with McCaffery's claim that capitalism has carried out the goal of the avant-grade—the abolition of total structure. But Andrews hardly agrees that such a development is positive. The political activity of the avant-garde now lies elsewhere, as we shall see.

One could ask, however, how a passage from a poem of Andrews's such as the following resists the homogenization he warns against in the above:

SONG NO 129

```
waldio        draig        impyn
                             holl
                           bronwen    pos
     plisgo      hafan
nodachfa
        oed         santes   rhwd
                              illawcio
                                        sarn
                                  heulog
                              haig
                              achul   can
                          job
gweithfa   balm              canolwar
oen      nodd
rewyddiaduriaeth
                              blaenori   tref
                          tramgwyddo
tosyn     wele       reiat
cynffon   maint
medi
```

Andrews's answer is that "Whether we bypass the referential fetish by writing non-signs or whether we tackle & problematize it depends, again, on how we define the medium. Writing is actually constitutive of these underlying libidinal flows; it is the desire for meaning, if not message. This is a third characterization of the medium, acknowledging the usefulness of the second one but acknowledging its limitations also" (*LB*, 135). Writing is neither simply *representation* nor *repression;* it is, Andrews claims, the *production* of meaning and value. These meanings can be reinforced (realism), blown apart (structuralism), or opposed by a "political writing that unveils demystifies the creation & sharing of meaning." Andrews wants a practice through which the production of meaning can be felt, not just taken for granted or destroyed. While only "a dramatic change in the structure of capitalist society is likely to disorganize the fetish" (p. 136), poets in the meantime can draw attention to the ideological structuration of sign systems. Andrews's poem above is to be seen, then, as precisely such a focus on the building blocks and processes that go into any organization of signs into semes through the manipulation of syllables (here quite typical Anglo-Saxon ones) and space, as well as the constitution of desires, the "articulation of and on the body" ("Constitution," 163). His concern with the body in the poem, reminiscent of Foucault's body politics, can be seen in the performance instructions which accompany many of the poems in *Love Songs,* such as those for "NO 117": *"Two performers walking, the first slowly, the second swiftly, repeating their word (memorized). . . .*

Each time A crosses the path of B (the closer the better), both performers go on to the next word."

A further distinction between Andrews's concern with the production of meaning and that of a purely structuralist linguistics is his insistence that "systems of meaning . . . [are] broader than signification, broader than the structure of the sign, but something more like 'sense' or 'value' in a more social dimension" ("Total Equals What," 48). While the structuration of ideology and social organization can be seen as analogous to the structuration of language, it should not be reduced to the latter. Though the structuralist focus on the immanent process of signification helps one to see the epistemological problems of realist modes of discourse, Andrews claims that that is only one level or horizon of language. A second horizon can be seen as "the structure of discourse" which organizes the diacritical differences of signification into a polyphony of voices and puts those differences "in motion, through action, through the organization of desire, through the organization of discourse" (p. 49). The third and ultimate linguistic horizon is the set of ideologies which "inscribe in different ways" the polyphonic organization of differences. Thus, a particular ideological formation structures the limits and possibilities of discursive practices.

The exploration and explanation of the possibilities for meaning, then, serve also as a critique of ideological and social practices. For the materials of language, through their particular articulation, are transformed into meaning—a meaning which though arbitrary in Saussure's sense is nevertheless imposed, distinctions organized into interdependency, each requiring the other "as the ground of their possibility" ("Total Equals What," 52). This recognition should not lead to the abandonment of organization, Andrews argues, but instead to a more positive recognition of possibility:

> By calling attention to possibility, we're acknowledging that the totality [in Althusser's sense] isn't just a negative restrictive thing, or some deterministic program. It's also something that's reproduced by action within the system and, at the same time, it becomes a resource or a medium that can be drawn upon. . . . The social rules that are involved in it are positive, enabling, constructive, and constitutive. . . . To imagine the limits of language (as an active process, a method) is also to imagine the limits of a whole form of social life—in this case, of a predatory social order (or interlocking network of orderings) that desperately needs to be changed. ("Total Equals What," 53)

A poetry that is critical, demythologizing, contextualizing (in the sense of recognizing the codes giving shape to language) can become an active intervention as a laying bare of the device, an uncovering of the framing involved in any meaning, a framing which both sets limits and offers possibilities, extensions, alternatives.

In this way Andrews suggests a way out of the endless debate between realism and modernism. The focus of the debate has shifted, the terms now being modernism versus "a more social [or socialist] perspective." The question, no longer about representation-vs.-repression, now is "whether form, as an activity, will help reinforce the generative qualities of language's raw materials rather than close it off" (p. 57). Such a question implies a way of looking at Andrews's "SONG NO 129" above as revealing the resonating, generative potential of language in addition to its more negative role as ideology critique. Andrews proposes a practice, then, which desires both openness and possibility.

To return to our initial question, then, of the whether to which Andrews and Bernstein might identify with the position which Eagleton satirizes (and supposing, as I do, that Andrews and Bernstein share a close enough position not to complicate such a question), the answer is both yes and no. To the extent that the *Tel Quel* position questions the hegemony of realism as a literary and epistemological mode of representation in capitalist society, then the editors of $L=A=N=G=U=A=G=E$ would agree. But to the extent that it offers no possibility of practice *within* language—there being no constructive possibility of a purely genotextual mode of praxis—Andrews and Bernstein in a qualified way share Eagleton's suspicion that history has somehow evaporated from such a view.

To what extent Andrews and Bernstein share Eagleton's call for a "materialist realist" (" 'Aesthetics and Politics'," 31), who gives off a sense of "the dust and heat of the class struggle" (p. 33), is not clear. Eagleton's prescription is vague and uncomfortably romantic. The question, at any rate, cannot be between one mode of realism and another, for realism implies the representation of what can no longer be thought of as present in the first place. "Realism" remains endlessly trapped within questions of the paradigmatic axis of language. The shift that Andrews proposes is one to the syntagmatic axis, the site of framing or structuration. The question now is the social organization of the chain of signifiers within specific and determinate discourses. Praxis is now a question of syntaxis.

FIVE

Praxis and Syntaxis

Ideology and the Economy of Space

> "There is no such thing as an empty space or
> an empty time."
>   —John Cage

In "Language, Realism, Poetry," the introduction to *In the American Tree,* Ron Silliman writes, "As is manifestly clear in the pages that follow, neither speech nor reference were ever, in any real sense, 'the enemy' " (p. xvi). In "Semblance" Charles Bernstein writes, "Not 'death' of the referent—rather a recharged use of the multivalent referential vectors that any word has . . ." (*The L=A=N=G=U=A=G=E Book,* 115; hereafter *LB*). In "Text and Context" Bruce Andrews notes, "Not exactly 'dereferentialist'—for can writing be adequately tagged with what it's not doing? Isn't that the old chest-busting negativism of the avant-garde?" (*LB,* 31). And Andrews and Bernstein together insist, in "Repossessing the Word," that "the idea that writing should (or could) be stripped of reference is as bothersome and confusing as the assumption that the primary function of words is to refer, one-on-one, to an already constructed world of 'things.' Rather, reference, like the body itself, is one of the horizons of language, whose value is to be found in the writing (the world) before which we find ourselves at any moment" (*LB,* ix).

The momentum behind such qualifications grows out of the desire of many so-called Language poets to break out of the anti-referentialist stereotype within which they have been defined. They themselves, of course, are largely responsible for such a characterization because of their earlier realism-equals-reification argument and their participation in symposia such as "The Politics of the Referent" (1977) and "The Death of the Referent?" (1981), the question mark in the latter title notwithstanding. Whether or not it is true that "reference . . . is one of the horizons of language" (Jacques Derrida's work at the very least challenges such a claim), it is important to examine the *reasons* some of these poets give for rejecting the stereotype of anti-referentialist. As the above statements indicate; the poets do not want to limit the scope of language nor to act out of pure negativity. They instead wish to *expand* the scope of language and to present a *positive* front in their challenge to common linguistic assumptions.

"The recent non-referential formalists, such as Clark Coolidge and Robert Grenier," writes Silliman, "frontally attack referentiality, but only through negation by specific context. To the extent that negation is determined by the thing negated, they too operate within the referential fetish" (*LB*, 131). The early work of Coolidge, Grenier, McCaffery, Andrews, and Silliman all served as the logical extension of the dominant focus of literary art in bourgeois society—the paradigmatic. Saussure, as we have seen, divided *parole* or the spoken utterance into two axes, the paradigmatic and the syntagmatic or, as Roman Jakobson later called them, the metaphoric and the metonymic ("Two Aspects of Language"). The paradigmatic axis refers to the word's "vertical" relation to a given *langue*, all other words which could be associated with or substituted for the word, as in metaphor when one word stands in for another. The paradigmatic axis also represents the possible connotations of the word and, ultimately, the word's signified. Questions of reference, then, examine the paradigmatic extensions of the sign. The syntagmatic axis, in contrast, refers to the word's "horizontal" relation to other words around it, as in a sentence, the chain of contiguous signifiers. It is the syntagmatic axis which limits the possible connotations on a given word's paradigmatic axis.

While the so-called anti-referential poem is posed as an attempt to deny the possibility of reference, it nevertheless remains within the paradigmatic approach to poetry. But once the question of reference has been bracketed, new possibilities for the conception of the poem arise. It is the achievement of many Language poets to think beyond the stalemate of the paradigmatic question and to pose poetry as an exploration of the syntagmatic, as a question of the power of frames and, by extension (as we shall see), of ideology. The role of poetry thus shifts from denying to revealing, unveiling, dis-covering.

In order to follow this important shift in focus from the paradigmatic to the syntagmatic, I will first explore the assumptions inherent in a paradigmatic focus. Next I will look at the discussion of syntax initiated by the minimalist and conceptual artists and its influence on certain Language poets' expanded notion of poetic syntax. And then I will follow that exploration with a reading of particular Language works that are built on these notions of expanded syntax, and the political claims that arise from the process which could be called "syntaxis": the act of laying bare the role of syntactical frames in ideological production.

Extensions of the Paradigm

As Silliman explains in "Surprised By Sign (Notes on Nine)," Roland Barthes's *Writing Degree Zero*, though written about French poets such as René Char, applies quite well to the Language poets represented in "The Dwelling Place" anthology of 1975 (the title itself coming from a phrase in Barthes's book). Consequently, since my assertion that some modern poetry underscores the syntagm rather than the paradigm appears to contradict Barthes's discussion, I first need to address myself to the claims of *Writing Degree Zero*. In characterizing the shift in poetry that has occurred since Rimbaud, Barthes emphasizes the breakdown of syntax and the foregrounding of the word's materiality in modern poems. Whereas Barthes sees classical poetry as a decorative form of prose, both modes performing the same expressive function, modern poetry by contrast appears to be written in a language quite foreign to prose. The word in a classical poem was a function, a transparency; the word in the modern poem is a substance, an object *sui generis*. In modern poetry, Barthes explains:

> . . . connections only fascinate. . . . the Word in poetry can never be untrue, because it is a whole; it shines with an infinite freedom and prepares to radiate towards innumerable uncertain and possible connections. Fixed connections being abolished, the word is left only with a vertical project, it is like a monolith, or a pillar which plunges into a totality of meanings, reflexes and recollections: it is a sign which stands. The poetic word is here an act without an immediate past, without environment, and which holds forth only the dense shadow of reflexes from all sources which are associated with it. Thus under each Word in modern poetry there lies an existential geology. (p. 40)

By "project" Barthes may mean that the word extends only on its vertical axis (projection) or that the word's goal now is only to foreground its vertical, referential dimension. In either case he overlooks that the effect of the isolate word is not simply a focusing on the paradigmatic extensions due to its unanchored position in an indeterminate syntax but, more important, a reflection on the role of syntax itself in determining the particular coloring of a word. To say, furthermore, that such a word is now without environment (syntactical context) is to impose an unnecessarily narrow definition onto the word "environment." No word, even the word which appears by itself on an otherwise blank page, is without environment; it is simply without its normative environment. Barthes restricts himself to the paradigmatic extensions of the poem; but it is the syntagmatic extension which concerns many Language poets.

Certainly Barthes is not unusual in his focus on the referential vectors of the word, for that has long been the focus of questions about language. But the works of Lyn Hejinian, Carla Harryman, Bruce Andrews, Charles Bernstein, and other Language poets are not simply (or not always) a negative reaction to the domination of the paradigmatic; those works begin a thinking outside of purely paradigmatic concerns. In order to see this shift, we first need to explore (by means of what may at first seem an infinite digression through the history of literary theory) the possibilities of poetic form within such vertical concerns. For only then will the particular contribution of the Language poets be clear.

A good starting point is the Romantic challenge to late eighteenth-century mimetic modes. The dominant poetic modes available to the eighteenth- and nineteenth-century British poet were reflection and expression. Whereas empiricist philosophy led to the valorization of art as a reflection (a mirror) of the external world, the idealist philosophies of Kant, and later Hegel among others, led to the emphasis on the expression of the Imagination (a lamp) which to a greater or lesser extent colored one's perception of the external. In either case, however, the emphasis is on the mediation between perception and reality, subject and object, an epistemological or paradigmatic concern; while the nature of the medium is questioned, the essential grounds of the debate are not.

With the aid of semiologist A. J. Greimas's "semantic rectangle," however, we should be able to flesh out other possibilities extending from this initial binary opposition between representation and expression. Such a semiotic system could be schematized as follows:

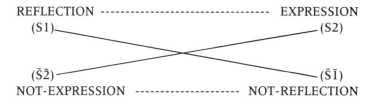

REFLECTION ------------------------------- EXPRESSION
(S1)   (S2)

(S̄2̄)   (S̄1̄)
NOT-EXPRESSION -------------------- NOT-REFLECTION

In "The Interaction of Semiotic Constraints" Greimas and F. Rastier explain that any given seme (S1) implies its contrary (S2), even when that contrary is unstated. Any seme, in other words, is always one pole in a binary opposition. But that seme also implies its contradiction (S̄1̄) as well as the contradiction of its contrary (S̄2̄). When the question of the subject/object relationship dominates aesthetics, as it did in the late eighteenth century and beyond, then the possibilities for various aesthetic modes will grow out of that dominant question. Those possibilities result from the combination of two contiguous poles of the semantic rectangle, such as S1 with S2, S1 with S̄2̄, S2 with S̄1̄, or S̄2̄ with S̄1̄; or as I have charted these possibilities above, Reflection with Expression, Reflection with Not-Expression, Expression with Not-Reflection, and Not-Expression with Not-Reflection, respectively.

Romanticism, though it tended to emphasize the expressive pole, must be seen as the combination of Reflection and Expression, as an attempt to mediate between both perceptual models. In "Lines Written a Few Miles above Tintern Abbey" William Wordsworth himself emphasizes the necessity of both poles, his interest lying in "eye and ear, both what they half-create,/ And what perceive; well pleased to recognize/ In nature and the language of the sense,/ The anchor of my purest thoughts. . . ." M. H. Abrams also stresses this reciprocity in *The Mirror and the Lamp*, claiming that for the Romantics "poetry is an interaction, the joint effect of inner and outer, mind and object, passion and the perceptions of sense" (p. 51). Various Romantic metaphors for poetic creation (like the lamp) are "analogies of projection into, or reciprocity with, elements from without" (p. 62). Neo-classicism and, later, realism and naturalism could all be plotted, on the other hand, as the resolution of the axes of Reflection and Not-Expression. Abstract expressionism could be plotted between Expression and Not-Reflection, and minimalism between Not-Expression and Not-Reflection. In terms of a paradigmatic emphasis, then, minimalism would be one of the most negative manifestations possible. I would chart these combinations as follows:

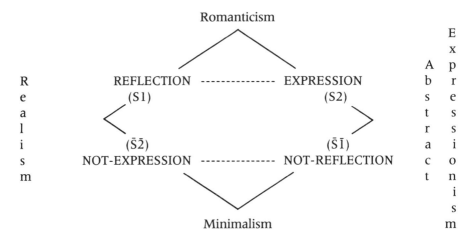

As we shall see, the Language poets extend their aesthetic and political considerations beyond the limits of these four combinations. That extension results from these poets' turn to art theory.

The attention above to labels usually applied to schools of visual art, then, is not gratuitous. The work of the New York School poets has often been explained in terms derived from abstract expressionist painting. Jack Kerouac's *Visions of Cody* as well as Clark Coolidge's early work draw on abstract expressionist concerns, such as the primacy of ejaculatory expression without concern for the resulting form, as seen in Kerouac's spontaneous bop prosody and Coolidge's concern with jazz rhythms. (See the latter's *A Note on Bop*.) Just so, much early Language poetry was described in terms heavily influenced first by the critical discussions of minimal sculpture and then by the discussions of conceptual art. In order to understand the relevance of these art discourses to early works and critical claims by various Language poets, as well as to the question of paradigmatic concerns, we first need to examine the claims of minimalist and conceptual artists of the sixties and early seventies. It is in this art theory that one can best see the shift from a paradigmatic frame to a syntagmatic one.

A typical minimal art work might consist of a six-foot white cube placed on the floor of an otherwise empty, all-white room. In this example both reflection and expression have been effaced. Whereas reflection leads the viewer to pass through a work to something other, as in looking "through" stone in order to see a body in an ancient Greek sculpture, the white cube represents nothing other than itself, its "cubeness," its material. It functions, in other words, as a material signifier. And whereas expression leads the viewer to read the work as the result of the artist's emotion or genius, positing an internal symbolic space, the white cube makes such a reading difficult. The white cube instead stands as an object, an arrangement of surface relations, a presence to be negotiated as the viewer walks around it, viewing it from all angles. "Minimal Art," painter Allen Leepa writes, "focuses on sensations based on direct perception of objects, which in painting are the lines, colors, planes, forms, and not on symbolic interpretation of them, as when a line is used to express a subjective emotional state of the artist" ("Minimal Art and Primary Meaning," 203). And therein lies the major distinction between minimalism and abstract expressionism.

The interaction between the gallery space, the object itself, and the viewer's body becomes the focus of the minimal sculpture, all seen in relation to one another within a perceptual field. In order to emphasize this focus, the work is pared down to its bare minimum of object-features, a kind of phenomenological reduction to a pure geometry of spatial perception. Our six-foot cube, as sculptor Robert Morris points out in "Notes on Sculpture" (1966), is different from every side. "The constant shape of the cube held in the mind but which the viewer never literally experiences, is an actuality against which the literal changing, perspective views are related. There are two distinct terms: the known constant and the experienced variable" (p. 234). The size of the object, furthermore, as with our six-foot cube, forces the viewer into an awareness of his or her own body as an object in space in a relationship with other bodies. If the cube were significantly smaller, the viewer may not become aware of these relationships; if it were larger, he or she may be overwhelmed, feel insignificant when the point is to feel in-relation-to.

As this stress on bodies in space suggests, minimal art, though negative in terms of reflection and expression, is far from negative in its ultimate claims. "It is not surprising," Morris writes, "that some of the new sculpture . . . has been called negative, boring, nihilistic" (p. 235). But such judgments imply a desire to find meaning *within* the object. The point of minimal sculpture is to expand the reading of the work outward from the object into the world. Here we see the beginning of a concern with an expanded notion of syntax which, although it remains within a primarily phenomenological or paradigmatic concern with subject and object, offers some Language poets a way into the question of the role of frames in constituting our experiences. Minimalism, then, can be seen as the site of transition from paradigmatic to syntagmatic concerns.

Because of its influence on minimalist thought, Merleau-Ponty's notion of "intercorporeal communication" is key to this transition. In expanding Husserl's concepts of intentionality (our ability to imagine the total cube when facing it from only one angle) and horizon (the limits of our perception of the cube, of our intentionality) from a concern with purely ideational objects to physical ones, Merleau-Ponty posits a language of the body or, more accurately, of bodies. We no longer look at a work and try to read the phenomenological horizon of the artist, as phenomenologist Georges Poulet would do. Instead we focus on the perceptual field in which the work sits as a material presence. In "The Philosopher and His Shadow" Merleau-Ponty explains "that the body is a 'perceiving thing,' a 'subject-object.' . . . space itself is known through my body. . . . When we say that the perceived thing is grasped 'in person' or 'in the flesh' . . . , this is to be taken literally: the flesh of what is perceived, this compact particle which stops exploration, and this optimum which terminates it all reflect my own incarnation and are its counterpart" (pp. 166–67). We are engaged in a language with the objects around us, he claims, our bodies in motion establishing a complex "syntax," so to speak, a redistribution of objects in space. Meaning is not sought within the objects themselves but in the fact of their pure presence and their relationships to other object-presences. Merleau-Ponty's phenomenological reduction, then, is not an attempt to extinguish meaning but instead to lay bare the basic units of perception responsible for meaning.

Poets of the Syntagmeme

Steve McCaffery, in "The Death of the Subject" (1976), extends Merleau-Ponty's metaphysics of presence to his own minimalist conception of language-centered poetry. And just like minimalist sculpture, McCaffery's minimalist poetics can be seen as an attempt to transform its initial negative rejection of reflection and expression into a more positive concern with the basic elements necessary for meaning. The result, however, is an ambiguous fusion of both negative and positive impulses. His negative response to the notion of reference is clear in the essay's subtitle, "The Implications of Counter-Communication in Recent Language-Centered Writing." If communication is unequivocally related to commodity fetishism—and we have seen in the last chapter that McCaffery sees such a relationship—then one obvious reaction is to write a poetry that refuses to communicate. McCaffery does this by reducing the sign to the cipher (his term for what I have been calling the material signifier). Like the minimal sculpture which no longer refers beyond itself, the cipher is an object to be negotiated rather than evaporated through the act of reading. In opposition to the notion of the cipher as simply a meaning fragment waiting for completion, McCaffery hopes that readers will approach the cipher as a graphemic presence, a phenomenological immediacy freed from the repressive constraints of a predetermined syntax. Readers themselves will then be free to arrange the various "presences" of the poem in any or all possible combinations. Through such language-centered (as opposed to referent-centered) writing, reading becomes writing.

But if, as McCaffery claims, meaning is a fetish and syntax an oppressive constraint, then this writing does not escape those problems. The role of oppressor is simply shifted from the writer to the reader in a curious form of what Freud calls the return of the repressed. Negation, as we have seen, depends on that which is negated. But the signs of a partial resolution to this problem appear in McCaffery's more positive claim for this poetic mode. His claim, like that of phenomenology, is that such linguistic reduction fore-grounds the role of syntactical frames in the creation of meaning, thereby making the reader more conscious of the framing process itself. Hence "a new concept of the meaningful" [p. 12] in which "the spatial placement of the graphemes and the sheer fact of their density" are to be seen as an expanded notion of syntax. "Syntax is transformed to become a calculus of densities and a geomantic ordering of pure experiences" [p. 13].

What does such a "calculus of densities" look like? McCaffery cites a poem of his own:

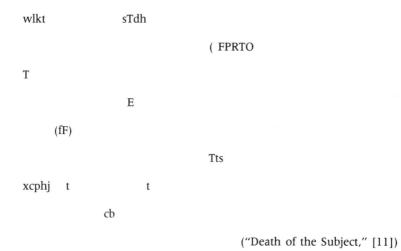

("Death of the Subject," [11])

The analogy between the descriptions of minimal sculpture and poetry such as this becomes clear in McCaffery's description of the minimal poem. Just as in sculpture where the gallery room is seen as a field in which presences sit in a spatial relation to each other and to the shape of the room itself—negative space thus signifying as much as the objects within it—so the page of the minimal poem here is to be seen as a field in which graphematic presences sit in various relationships to one another. In such a poem "there is a striking non-gravitational effect . . . that rises from the multiple interlocking of parts and the replacement of linear direction by a vertical and horizontal balancing which creates a tracery in spatial neutrality and highlights the coronal nature of the graphemes" [p. 14]. One could expand on McCaffery's reading as follows: The capital T in the above poem can be seen as a nexus of radiating vectors which connect it to the other letter combinations. Its capitalization as well as its spatial location relate it to the capital E below it. Its T-ness, on the other hand, relates it to the letter clusters above it, which all contain Ts, as well as to the group of lower case and upper case Ts in "Tts" and the individual lower case Ts farther below. Among its other graphemic qualities (such as the use of parentheses), then, the poem is organized—or perhaps I should say my reading organizes the poem—around the letter T.

Ironically, the conception of syntax needed to read McCaffery's poem depends on an analogy to "readings" of sculptural syntax. And those readings of sculpture depend on a prior analogy to language. The result of such a circular route is *a* language based on an analogy to *language* in general. We are not yet finished, then, with our excursion into the visual arts, for the particular form that such a metalanguage takes in the development of some Language poetry is partly determined by the metalanguage arrived at by various Conceptual artists from the mid-1960s to the early 1970s. In addition to being a Conceptual artist, for instance, Vito Acconci coedited the poetry magazine *0–9* (1967–1969) with Bernadette Mayer, the latter having taught some of the Language poets at the St. Mark's poetry workshop in New York as well as having her own work in $L=A=N=G=U=A=G=E$ magazine and in the anthology *In the American Tree*.

The Conceptualists' turn to language extended the process of abstraction which seemed already to have reached its limits in minimalism. Conceptualism grew out of the recognition that the reduction which the minimalists hoped for, the realization of a pure formal geometry, was subverted by the adherence to material objects. Geometry, after all, is a conceptual construct which may or may not be applied to matter. In order to understand what has been applied, furthermore, viewers of minimal sculpture need to learn a new language which extends aesthetic value to a new array of objects previously excluded from the realm of art. Whether an object is to be labeled "art," the Conceptualists claimed, depends on the values of a particular, defined aesthetic context—on a particular art language.

The Conceptualists were thus carrying on the self-conscious art practice begun by Duchamp with his ready-mades. Duchamp's exhibition of his "Fountain," as we have seen, was an attempt to lay bare the socially-determined context—the gallery—which conferred art status on objects exhibited therein. To the extent that minimalists remained dependent on gallery space in order to make their syntactic claims (not all minimal art appeared in galleries, of course), the Conceptualists saw them (the minimalists) as extending, but not significantly challenging, that particular context. The Conceptualists therefore often presented their work in other contexts such as meadows, deserts, and books. Furthermore, since Minimalists remained tied to objects, they participated in the socially contrived illusion that art depends on material, material that could be appropriated and commodified by the art market. The Conceptualists therefore turned to less "material" matter, such as water, inert gas, or ultimately simply ideas, in a process of increasing "dematerialization" of art. The original conception, the idea, the intention of the artist *is* the art work.

"Declaration" thus becomes the determining context of art. Echoing Duchamp, the Conceptualists claimed that anything is art if you call it art. This claim leads to "works" such as Terry Atkinson's and Michael Baldwin's *Declaration Series* (1967), one part of which was their declaration that Oxfordshire was now to be thought of as an art milieu. Objects within Oxfordshire would automatically attain art status. But how does one view or experience Oxfordshire or a square mile of ocean water in an undetermined location or a particular amount of invisible gas as an art work? These works depended first on their declaration and then on their documentation through photographs and written descriptions (which sometimes ended up on museum walls in place of the "work"). Art was thus translated from a material mode to a propositional mode, claimed Ian Burn and Mel Ramsden in *The Grammarian* (1970): now "artwork may be largely contingent upon getting one's language straight. Consequently it may be formalizable: i.e., one of the functions of Conceptual Art may now be to sort out some basic semiotic guides or rules" (cited in Meyer's *Conceptual Art*, 100). It was this turn to semiotic questions, as well as to the various writing modes developed by the conceptualists (declaration, self-interrogation, performance instructions, documentation, and axiomatic proposition), which proved most important in the Language poets' application of conceptualism to poetry.

The step from conceptual art to "conceptual" poetry should seem quite natural since the turn from object to language places the visual artist in what is already the domain of poetry—the exploration of language. One significant difference between conceptual art and conceptual poetry, however, is that the artists' shift from their own medium (visible matter) to a foreign medium (language) perhaps cannot be achieved in poetry. What medium other than language can poetry take place in? Since poetry already takes place through language, Barrett Watten claims, it "takes into account a more significant 'resistance of the medium' than does Conceptual Art—which is often simply a projection of the category 'art' . . . onto phenomena outside the order of art. There can be no 'conceptual' poetry; I can think of no example of a poet transferring the designation 'poetry' onto materials without providing for an interior structure" (*Total Syntax*, 217). Of course someone *could* do so, claiming that Watten's notion of poetry, which rests solely on a set of conventions, does not allow for the possibility that anything can be thought of as having an interior structure once we "declare" that such is the case. There is nothing except social convention, one could argue, that prevents us from extending the category "poetry" to anything we choose, whether or not Watten can think of such an example. Nevertheless, the value of this extension is not at all clear, since the value of the extension of "art" lies specifically in its recognition of conventions as particular languages through which particular objects or conceptions can be included or excluded from the category "art." From this perspective, poetry already exists within the privileged medium.

At any rate, the conceptual artists offered the Language poets a model of exploration which has proven quite valuable in coming to terms with the social implications of syntax; but it is the extent to which both question the social implications of poetic assumptions and conventions that distinguishes many Language poets from many conceptualists. The latter's recognition of the restrictive nature of art languages led many conceptualists to attempt to free art from such restrictions by breaking it out of those confines. The end result is that, as conceptualist Joseph Kosuth puts it, "art indeed exists for its own sake" (*Conceptual Art,* 170). In his discussion of the Art-Language group Watten explains: "There is no critique of motivation, neither for objects nor for frames. Rather, Art-Language builds only from the outside of already existing objects and frames. Its language can only contradict their ontology; it does not know how to change their meaning. The only meaning given by Art-Language is 'not this': the significant contradiction of the Romantic" (*Total Syntax,* 215). The role of any meaningful extension of "poetry," Watten implies, would then be to critique the motivation of objects and frames. In other words, it is not enough simply to identify frames; one must also ask where those frames come from and whose interests they serve.

Silliman's work often reveals his concern with the social motivation of frames. While the form of much of his work resembles the propositional mode of the conceptualists, as we shall see, he nevertheless insistently extends the focus of those propositions to a more consciously political level than many conceptualists would have. Silliman's *The Chinese Notebook* (in *The Age of Huts,* 41–66), for instance, provides a useful counter to Sol LeWitt's "Sentences on Conceptual Art" (1968), which begins as follows:

1) Conceptual Artists are mystics rather than rationalists. They leap to conclusions that logic cannot reach.
2) Rational judgments repeat rational judgments.
3) Illogical judgments lead to new experience.
4) Formal art is essentially rational.
5) Irrational thoughts should be followed absolutely and logically.

While the matter-of-fact, axiomatic mode of statement, the self-referring content, the numbering of passages, and the sentence-by-sentence progression of LeWitt's "Sentences" all influence the format of Silliman's *The Chinese Notebook,* their content is quite different. Whereas Silliman will echo a statement of LeWitt's such as "17) All ideas are art if they are concerned with art and fall within the conventions of art," he will counter other claims such as "24) Perception is subjective."

Silliman's first proposition reveals his attention to and expansion of conceptualist claims:

> 1. Wayward, we weigh words. Nouns reward objects for meaning. The chair in the air is covered with hair. No part is in touch with the planet.

His attention to the materiality of words—in that only the words on the page can help one to distinguish between "wayward" and "weigh word"—immediately complicates the conceptualist claim to have finally got beyond the material by turning to language. The sentences that follow, furthermore, bring up the question of reference (which the conceptualists tended to ignore) while also mimicking the conceptualist work which can only exist in the mind. In propositon two, however, Silliman complicates the latter point as well:

> 2. Each time I pass the garage of a certain yellow house, I am greeted with barking. The first time this occurred, an instinctive fear seemed to run through me. I have never been attacked. Yet I firmly believe that if I opened the door to the garage I should confront a dog.

A perfect example of the conceptualist technique—we "conceive" of the dog which not only has never been seen behind the door but also never appears in this proposition until the final word. But unlike the conceptualist declaration, this proposition carries consequences should there in fact be a dog ready to attack from behind the door. Silliman seems to imply the practical need for being able to conceive of the dog even though in other situations (as in race discrimination) the dependence on categories may be socially harmful—not all conceptions carry the same implications.

Silliman's propositions in contrast to LeWitt's carry an explicitly political charge. According to proposition five: "Language is, first of all, a political question." Silliman is not merely looking for a way to purify poetic language; even the metalanguage of the declaration carries political implications:

> 7. This is not philosophy, it's poetry. And if I say so, then it becomes painting, music or sculpture, judged as such. If there are variables to consider, they are at least partly economic—the question of distribution, etc. Also differing critical traditions. . . .

No declaration, Silliman implies, exists outside of social frames such as economic structures and critical traditions; the declaration is marked by those conditions even when hoping to transcend them.

The awareness of context, in other words, takes place within a particular context. Even so, that awareness of context is indispensible, a perpetual reflexiveness to guard against the following:

> 32. The Manson family, the SLA. What if a group began to define the perceived world according to a complex, internally consistent, and precise (tho not accurate) language? Might not the syntax itself propel reality to such a point that to our own they could not return? Isn't that what happened to Hitler?

As a counter to Hitler's atrocities Silliman seeks a constant attention to the necessity for, yet arbitrariness of, ideological frames. Therein lies the role of the "poets of the syntagmeme" (proposition 44).

One way of laying bare the frame is to submit some constant (a word, phrase, sentence) to perpetual recontextualization. Through such a process the given constant takes on quite different connotations in different contexts. Bob Perelman's "Before Water" (7 *Works*, 53–66), reminiscent of Gertrude Stein's characteristic mode, recontextualizes a number of different constants through a process of reiteration in which nothing is repeated in exactly the same way. Perelman has suggested in correspondence that in the poem he is "trying to enact the birth of signification," which he does in both content and form. The recurrence of key words throughout establishes and complicates the theme of signification. In fact, this complication begins with the title itself: does "before" refer to place or time? "Before" as a preposition indicating a spatial relationship could refer to the speaker standing before water, fronting the external world which exists beyond or prior to signification, an object waiting for a name. If "before" indicates a temporal relationship, however, quite a different view of signification is implied: the word comes first, itself constituting (framing) water through the act of naming. In fact, both of these senses seem to occur simultaneously, establishing a tension and an ambiguity which determines the protean shifts of terms from line to line. The signified of these key signifiers—sentence, world, sound, water, noise, vocabulary, thought, sense, mind, edge, I, blue—shifts as the syntax of each new line shifts, each new incoming wave establishing a new relationship to the shoreline.

This series of 395 relatively discrete lines with no end punctuation establishes an intense rhythm, a temporal repetition that is at odds with the continuing shifts of the elements within the lines. The implication here is that although the perceiver is continually confronted with the same objects, each new instance of perception establishes a new relationship among these objects, underlining the protean and arbitrary nature of signification. Tracing one of these shifting constants, the word "blue," through the poem should illustrate this process:

> Blue over once one more noise (line 9)
> Water roll sense make blue (21)
> The clear blue birth of green (23)

Blue course no noise in this sentence (27)
Blue and noise at each edge of the sound (34)
Blue water at the sense's edge (42)
It's up to blue to say (47)
Each vocabulary contains its own blue (49)

In these eight lines the connections of the object, the vocalized noise, and sense gradually merge into signification, but the arbitrariness of this process is clear—where do we divide blue from green in the ocean? Later in the poem:

I say blue I see blue (236)
Blue and again it's water (241)
Blue nowhere outside of noise (257)
The blue line means water, the noise means blue (260)
Death gives blue noise out there (262)
Blue (265)
Green and blue or see into it (318)
No blue, no green, no water, itself complete (355)
A separated noise clears the way to blue (356)
See blue where blue was (362)

After this process of establishing signifiers which constitute signifieds (line 236), which divide the world into manageable abstractions (line 265) which nevertheless continue to be arbitrary (line 355), language comes into its own, drawing up the signified concept even if the referent is absent (line 362). At this point in the poem the individual lines are no longer bounded by the line breaks but can be formed into larger units: "The water roll as before/ Once it happens to sound outside all time/ The water sounds okay/ The noise crosses the sentence/ I'm ready to see/ It's water again" (ll. 390–95). This process remains ambiguous, however—does line 391 go with 390 or 392 or 392–95? All are possible, which is precisely the point.

The extension of possibilities for meaning appears in the work of the sculptor who has had the greatest impact on the Language school's exploration of syntax—Robert Smithson. Smithson's appeal, from his early minimalist work through his conceptualist period, is his exploration of expanded scale, frames, and metaphor. A photograph of his *Gyrostasis* (1968), for instance, appears on the cover of Douglas Messerli's anthology, *"Language" Poetries* (1987). Smithson's description of that sculpture reveals some of the concerns important to various Language poets:

The title GYROSTASIS refers to a branch of physics that deals with rotating bodies, and their tendency to maintain their equilibrium. The work is a standing triangulated spiral.

When I made the sculpture I was thinking of mapping procedures that refer to the planet Earth. One could consider it as a crystallized fragment of a gyroscopic rotation, or as an abstract three dimensional map that points to [Smithson's later work] the SPIRAL JETTY, 1970 in the Great Salt Lake, Utah. GYROSTASIS is relational, and should not be considered as an isolated object. (*The Writings of Robert Smithson,* 37).

The major point to recognize in Smithson's description is his interest in mapping phenomena which occur beyond direct perception, such as the rotation path of the earth or the objects of study of physics. In fact, the work of physicists, especially Niels Bohr's and Werner Heisenberg's recognition that only the development of a new language will provide scientists with the conceptual apparatuses needed to "map" newly discovered but imperceptible phenomena, has provided poet Nick Piombino with a mode of explaining the concerns of various Language poets. "Scientists and artists," Piombino writes, ". . . more and more realize that our whole grasp of experience is metaphorical. And now the new languages which scientists must speak in order to describe the future . . . have brought them closer to appreciating and finding use for imaginative expressions of linguistic transformation, not only in formal symbolic logic and mathematics, but also in the findings of poetry, art, and psychoanalysis" ("Towards an Experiential Syntax," 45).

Smithson's fascination with micro- and macroscopic fields leads him to an exploration of scale which lays bare the metaphoric nature of all scales and maps. His 1969 mirror displacements in the Yucatán (in which he places a series of square mirrors in various arrangements on the ground, often partially covering the mirrors with earth) are one example of his expansion of scale out of the museum, incorporating the earth itself into the work. This particular work, however, is largely ironic, a metaphor which plays on the notion that art holds a mirror up to nature. The varying positions of the mirrors are what produce the "reality" thereby reflected. Smithson insists that his work not be interpreted as an attempt to "get back to nature"; "nature" is merely one more value which serves to frame and delimit our experiences. "When the conscious artist perceives 'nature' everywhere," Smithson explains, "he starts detecting falsity in the apparent thickets, in the appearance of the real, and in the end he is skeptical about all notions of existence, objects, reality, etc." (*Writings,* 103). Such skepticism exposes the conventional frames.

Skepticism may also lead to a state of futility, however. "Minus Twelve" is a list of twelve categories, each with four subcategories, that evidently offer Smithson's views on the possibilities of art in contemporary society. "Minus Twelve" begins as follows:

1. USELESSNESS
    A. Zone of standard modules.
    B. Monoliths without color.
    C. An ever narrowing field of approximation.
    D. The circumscribed cube.

2. ENTROPY
   A. Equal units approaching divisibility.
   B. Something inconsistent with common experience or having contradictory qualities.
   C. Hollow blocks in a windowless room.
   D. Militant laziness.

(Writings, 81)

Smithson continues with the categories Absence, Inaccessibility, Emptiness, Inertia, Futility, Blindness, Stillness, Equivalence, Dislocation, and Forgetfulness. Smithson's "Minus Twelve" is ironic, however, for it is precisely qualities such as uselessness and entropy which give minimalist sculpture its value as a challenge to illusions about the normative concept of art. This irony has a positive dimension, as Barrett Watten explains in a discussion of Smithson's critical writings: "The realm of this literature is physical space; its constructive dimension is the illusion of time. The ironies of representation are located on the temporal axis, which is partial, entropic, and negative, while the affirmations of Smithson's method are space . . . where the ironies of the mind have been made physically real. Space implies a future which is not ironic" (*Total Syntax,* 81). Smithson's initial negative turn to entropy thus leads to a positive conception of space.

Language poet James Sherry, in his "Plus Thirteen" (*Popular Fiction,* 70–72), offers the positive translation that "Minus Twelve" implies. His first two sections, for instance, read as follows:

1. Usefulness
   a. Interlocking zones of varied configurations
   b. Colorful tools
   c. Precision of ambiguity
   d. Corral with the gate open
   e. Nourishment

2. Anti-entropic Forces
   a. Perception of subtle differences
   b. Events consistent with common experience
   c. Shape determining use
   d. Commitment
   e. Lazy arts

Sherry's implied criticism is that, while Smithson is correct in recognizing the positive side to entropy, the answer is not simply to give in to entropic forces but to put to use the attention to scale that the minimalists achieved. The "subtle perception of differences" can be a generative force, as Sherry's addition of a thirteenth section and a fifth subsection suggests. In contrast to Smithson's category 4C, "Toward an aesthetics of disappointment," Sherry offers "Toward the politics of language." The exploration of the economy of syntactic space, in its analogy to ideological framing, becomes for Sherry a form of political praxis.

Watten in particular has shown an interest in Smithson's work. The former's notion of "total syntax," for instance, grows partly out of his appreciation of Smithson's expanded scale. By "total syntax" Watten means an attention to both the internal, formal, temporal construction of a work and its external, contextual, spatial dimension. An artist structures a work within a particular conjunction of various external frames, such as aesthetic value-systems, economic constraints, and ideological structures—all of which impinge on the work in different ways. "The interior and exterior syntax are not separate," Watten claims; "rapidly they merge in the array of possibilities" of combination and contradiction (*Total Syntax*, 68). Smithson's work, then, in its denial of a temporal, internal development, accentuates the external conditions which shape it and which are in turn shaped by it. The gallery room or the Yucatán bush are as much constructed by the work as vice versa. On the other hand, Clark Coolidge's poetry such as *The Maintains* (1974), in its refusal to admit traditional poetic notions of reference, extends the possibilities of its internal play.

This dialectic of inside and outside structures Watten's book-length poem *Progress* (1986). The poem's format immediately challenges our conventional expectations for poetic syntax, as the first stanza illustrates:

> Relax,
>   stand at attention, and.
>   Purple snake stands out on
>   Porcelain tiles. The idea
> *Is* the thing. Skewed by design. . . .

The contradictory commands that open the poem set the stage for its overall structure of thesis and antithesis, through which our expectations for a continuous frame of reference are constantly undermined. Yet we are to heed the content of these lines as well: we need to learn to relax our conventional expectations of poetic form and to pay strict attention to the contextual permutations throughout. The question of frame and context then comes up more explicitly in the third and fourth lines as we perceive the snake against its background, their interdependence heightened by the alliteration of "purple snake" and "porcelain." The "stands out," furthermore, posits a different frame for the word "stand" than appears in the second line. In a proposition reminiscent of the conceptualists we hear that the idea is the thing, while the emphasis on context is driven home with the attention to the "design" of elliptical construction (which is nevertheless provisionally enclosed by the period following the ellipses).

The second stanza contrasts this notion of design with a more standardized one:

One way contradictory use is to
    Specify empty.
                    Basis, its
    Cover operates under insist on,
Delineate. Stalin as a linguist. . . .

A translation of the first two lines might be something like "One way to use contradiction is not to specify any particular context." That practice is contrasted to the one that seeks a more "stable" basis, but that basis, arbitrary in nature, will have to be insisted on by a more or less hidden police state of grammar and usage ("Stalin as a linguist"). Through the dissociative structure of the poem, however, such bases are constantly put into question. The hope is that the expansion of interior scale (through such unrelenting reflexivity) might in turn influence the exterior frames as well: "And unearthed in the process/ A form compelling events" (p. 7).

One specific event revealing such a form, Watten has suggested in conversation, was the Iranian hostage crisis during the Carter administration. Through the media's constant barrage of negative information concerning Carter's handling of the crisis in Iran, the American populace was forced to shift from one frame to another—from Carter's view of foreign policy which claimed to emphasize human rights abroad to another which insisted that, because of this previous policy, Americans were now victims to other nations. This event exposed the possibility of shifting frames, of seeing one frame (Carter's) as invalid, but did not lead to an exploration of the *function* of frames. The Carter frame was undermined while at the same time the ground was laid for another frame (namely Reagan's) suddenly to make sense, to appear as the obvious and only way to view current events. Watten's book *Progress,* on the other hand, continually calls into question each new frame which seeks to fill the gap left by the previous one.

This is not to say that *Progress* does not argue for a particular meta-frame in which to view frames. But Watten insists that any particular articulation of meta-frames can only be provisional, only locally valid: "I don't think there's any essential validity or invalidity to a form—what's important are its intentions and its particular negotiation with its time and place" ("Barrett Watten on Poetry and Politics," 203).

Michael Palmer's concern with recontextualization takes place in what could be called a verse of qualification. In poem after poem he explores the syntactical and logical conventions built into our language which serve to define a specific context for a topic. Those conventions—such as parenthesis, apposition, and conjunction—are submitted to a disorienting "defamiliarization," as the Russian Formalists called it, a constant positing and subverting of context. Palmer structures "The Village of Reason" (*First Figure*, 37–38), for example, around the contextualizing function of conjunction.

> This is a glove
> or a book from a book club

In this first stanza the poem begins with a shifter, as Jakobson and Benveniste call it, which fails to refer back to any specific antecedent. Is "this" the poem itself or some object to be identified within the poem? The conjunction "or" normally would clarify the situation a bit, but here it introduces even more complicating information.

Whatever partial resolution readers might impose upon the first stanza is likely to be challenged by the next:

> This is the sun
> or a layer of mud

The readers are given no clue as to whether the second "this" further qualifies the same object or refers to a new one, as in a list of objects. The ellipsis of the third stanza ("This is Monday,/ this an altered word") and the fourth stanza ("This is the village of reason/ and this an eye torn out") suggest that the poem presents a list of objects rather than a continuous qualification of one thing. But while the conjunction "and" serves to coordinate listed elements, it also serves to qualify the things listed by placing them in conjunction with one another: the "village of reason" is called into question by its association with "an eye torn out," suggesting that the connection between reason and perception is not absolute. In any case, the point is the fact of qualification, not the object qualified. A later stanza ("This is the mechanism/ and this the shadow of a bridge") emphasizes this point by reflexively drawing into consciousness the bridging mechanisms of the language.

Like Silliman's "parsimony principle," which states that readers will always take the path of least resistance by creating frames where no obvious frame exists, in "Lens" (*First Figure*, 9–10) Palmer suggests that readers will often bridge the gap between unrelated elements in a poem:

> I failed to draw a map and you followed it perfectly
> because the word 'cannot' inscribes itself here
> to define an atmosphere of absolute trust
> which both fastens and unfastens us.

The title suggests that the poem depends on the creation of perspective. Readers "trust" that such a perspective is provided to "fasten" the poet and audience within a specific "atmosphere." Whether such an experience is pleasant or unpleasant depends on the expectations of the perceiver:

The branches of the pine drooped heavily
in the moist air and this was pleasant
though at times it felt a little unpleasant
that he couldn't balance on his head

where the water trickled down the rocks.

Palmer next offers an example of the reader who bridges the gap between the available evidence and the possible meaning of the evidence:

He appears
to have seen the black pubic hair and the vagina
of a woman who squatted there to piss,
the gypsy nurse perhaps

who dealt in magic
holding the infant up with both hands.

Like Stephen Dedalus trying to mediate between the diaphane and the adiaphane in the "Proteus" episode of *Ulysses,* the speaker here tries to "read" the immediately visible conditions (perhaps the expression on someone's face). But the progression of that reading defies any immediately perceptible logic. Palmer continually undercuts the linearity of shifts from one perception to another.

He told
how gazing at a mountain pool

had induced a kind of waking sleep
which led to other things.
("I am the lover in the sense of dust"
were his exact words, spoken softly.)

The conventional function of parenthesis is to clarify a specific context, and certainly the "which led to other things" above calls out for clarification. But the parenthetical information which follows only leads us farther from any logical perspective that might help us organize this information. In what sense is a lover like dust? And why should "he" (whoever he is) speak softly? We are never told the answers, only that "the way/ did not matter, up or down,/ a few steps should be enough." The point is not where we are going, Palmer suggests, but that step by step we will get there, even without a map.

Conclusion

At this point we should be able to sketch an outline of the various possible poetic manifestations this concern with syntax offers. If, as I have suggested, some of the Language poets have provided a way of thinking outside of the paradigmatic frame, then we should be able to plot a new semantic rectangle based on a new initial binary opposition. Instead of the Reflection/Expression opposition which applies to questions of representation (Reflection as the representation of the external, Expression as that of the internal), I propose that the initial concerns of many "Language poets are Structure (as in frame, context, horizon) and Force (as in anything which resists structure: desire, play, impulse). Thus we could arrange the structure of possible permutations of this initial opposition as follows:

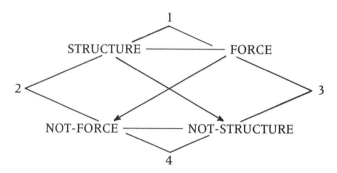

Within the syntagmatic paradigm, so to speak, the above four positions represent the range of possible stances toward the notions of Structure and Force. (I should mention here that I offer this schematic map as a way of asking questions about the stands of various poets on these issues, not as an end in itself.) The first position, then, represents the attempt to take into account both a concern with structure and a concern with force. I would argue that this is the position most often expressed by Andrews and Bernstein, the position I provisionally refer to as "syntaxis." By "syntaxis" I mean the mode of writing which, by baring the frame, deliberately focuses on the process of signification as a production of meaning through the syntactical organization of force. When Andrews states that his writing grows out of a "desire to investigate the possibilities of meaning, rather than just the possibilities of form—to investigate, in a sense, the way our ability to create different kinds of content and different kinds of form gets shaped" ("Total Equals What," 50), he is talking about writing as syntaxis. Bernstein posits similar concerns in the following: "What pulses, pushes, is energy, spirit, anima, dream, fantasy: coming out always in form, as shape" (LB, 44). The shape of energy, the structure of force: the two are never separate.

The second position on the chart above represents the emphasis on writing that focuses on the work's structure at the expense of the disruptive forces resisting that structure. Certain comments by Watten might lead one to place him here. His desire for "total syntax," for instance, might be interpreted in this light, as well as his desire to see that, "although the landscape is mutating, the driver is always in control of the car" (Total Syntax, 64). While such a reading of Watten's view might not be completely wrong, other of his statements complicate that reading. When Watten writes, for example, that for the contemporary writer "a thorough and uncompromising 'editorial' imagination is needed, alongside whatever dissociation participates in the original act" ("The XYZ of Reading," 4), he reveals a phase-one concern with the articulation of both structure and force. As he has told me in conversation, *Total Syntax* "implies an interest in extending the implications of art from the work into the world, but . . . also begs the questions of closure, totalization. . . . I'm not arguing for a totalization of art in political, psychological, or linguistic senses" ("Barrett Watten on Poetry and Politics," 196). It seems more accurate to place Watten along with Andrews and Bernstein in phase one while noting that phase one in fact offers a variety of possible articulations of structure and force. Phase one, as well as the other phases, should be depicted as a range of options between two extremes, as in the following extension of the preceding chart:

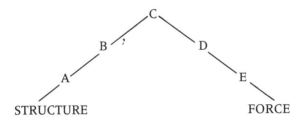

Thus we could say that Watten might appear at position 1A while Andrews might appear closer to 1D.

When Steve McCaffery calls for a poetry, on the other hand, built on the concern "for releasing energy flow, for securing the passage of libido in a multiplicity of flows out of the Logos" (*LB,* 88), he clearly articulates a position at the third phase. Here the emphasis is on the unrestrained flow of Force and the refusal to impose any obvious Structure whatsoever. But when he claims that "language centered writing not only codes its own flow but codes its own codicities," McCaffery reveals that—at least to some extent—he too works within the assumptions of phase one (perhaps at 1E). Nevertheless, his dominant position tends to be at phase three.

I cannot imagine what a poetry derived from phase four concerns would look like. Only the blank page would appear to meet the conditions of both Not-Force and Not-Structure, yet even the blank page can be read as the articulation of silence or refusal or death. "If the poet in Cocteau's Orpheus claims god-head by inscribing blank pages," Watten writes, "those pages still have been written—and if read aloud, they would have a temporal structure" (*Total Syntax,* 217). While the conceptualists have posited works which exist only in the mind, their position nevertheless is at phase one. Far from positing nothingness, they are profoundly concerned with ideational structure and content. And as we have suggested above, even the presentation of nothingness signifies.

At any rate, one aim of the above chart is to differentiate between various poets I have discussed throughout these chapters. But I wish to stress that even such a differentiation remains at a necessarily general level and does not imply that everyone who might be plotted at a certain point—say 1D—will write a similar poetry. That both Andrews and Bernstein could be said to occupy such a position does not at all imply that their poetry is then indistinguishable, or even that the poetry of each is homogeneous. The same poet can occupy different points at different times. As Douglas Messerli has pointed out in his introduction to the *"Language" Poetries* anthology, "If Andrews positions himself as a writer who would make his poetry a public production, . . . Bernstein advocates a concept of privacy for writing" (p. 4). My point is to identify particular articulations of concerns, of the claims that each poet makes for his or her poetry; to that extent, then, Andrews and Bernstein can be seen to be much closer in their views than each would be to Watten or Silliman or Howe.

Conversely, as I suggested in chapter one, the recognition that certain Russian Futurist poets and certain Language poets might write a poetry that looks similar does not guarantee that the concerns behind those poetries are at all similar. The effects of the formal characteristics of a poem depend on the intricate texture of contexts in which the poem is inscribed; the same poem may serve widely divergent ends at different times, among different audiences, within different historical contexts. This is my claim in chapter three against Jameson's reading of "China." His equation, however qualified, of schizophrenic language and Language poetry reveals an uncharacteristic insensitivity on Jameson's part to the role of context in determining the effects of a work. Jameson's uneasiness with any but a normative, narrative syntax might place him at phase two above.

My second aim in the chart and in this chapter is to emphasize the significance of the shift from predominantly paradigmatic concerns to syntagmatic ones. As I have said already, the work of some Language poets extends beyond a purely negative reaction within the paradigmatic horizon. If the claims of this poetry rested solely on those that I examine in chapter four—that this poetry subverts the referential fetish—then such a challenge, though important, would fail to point beyond the vertical axis.

It has been my hope in this chapter, however, to emphasize the positive challenge of this poetry—the challenge to question not just what we think but also the way we structure what we think. As I have suggested in chapter two, this challenge is an injunction not merely to think clearly but to recognize the role of ideological frames in the constitution of our world. Andrews makes this concern quite clear in the following: This poetry "moves toward a more critical (or contextual) focus on meaning itself and on . . . [an] overall social comprehension. And I think this involves a greater sensitivity to the matter of ideology—which is embodied in discursive frames that we use and in the social arrangements which stage the possibilities for meaning to be produced" ("Total Equals What," 50). That sensitivity to ideology lies in the manipulation of syntactical frames, in the creation of what Bernstein has called a "syntaxophony," in order first of all to lay bare the framing process of ideology; and second, to place the reader in a more active role as the coproducer of the meaning of the poem. Such a foregrounding of the "materialism of the idea," as Jacques Derrida has called it, through a conscious syntactical praxis is necessary in order to "counterbalance the neutralizing moments of any deconstruction" (*Dissemination,* 207). The important but neutralizing deconstruction of the "referential fetish"—and with it the bourgeois claim to "natural" language—must be accompanied by the laying bare of the framing process. Otherwise we simply substitute one realism for another and thereby perpetuate the very arbitrariness we criticize. The answer to reification is not a further obliteration of meaning—as McCaffery and Melnick have at times suggested—but a laying bare of the social process of meaning production. As Andrews puts it (*LB,* 136): "To politicize—not a closure but an *opening.*" Or as Marx puts it in *The Eighteenth Brumaire of Louis Bonaparte":* "The social revolution . . . cannot draw its poetry from the past, but only from the future."

Works Cited

Primary Works

Andrews, Bruce. "Constitution/Writing, Politics, Language, the Body." $L=A=N=G=U=A=G=E$ 4 (1981): 154–65, printed as *Open Letter,* fifth series, 4.
———. Excerpt from *I Don't Have Any Paper So Shut Up (Or, Social Romanticism).* *Temblor* 4 (1986): 67–74.
———. *Love Songs.* Baltimore: Pod, 1982. N. pag.
———. "Misrepresentation." $L=A=N=G=U=A=G=E$ 12 (vol. 3, no. 2) (1980): n. pag.
———. *Praxis.* Berkeley: Tuumba, 1978.
———. *Sonnets (Memento Mori).* Berkeley: This, 1980.
———. "Total Equals What: Poetics and Praxis." *Poetics Journal* 6 (1986): 48–61.
———. *Wobbling.* New York: Roof, 1981.
———. "Writing Social Work & Political Practice." $L=A=N=G=U=A=G=E$ 2.9/10 (October 1979): n. pag.
Andrews, Bruce, and Charles Bernstein, eds. $L=A=N=G=U=A=G=E$ 4 (1981), printed as *Open Letter,* fifth series, 4.
———. *The $L=A=N=G=U=A=G=E$ Book.* Carbondale: Southern Illinois University Press, 1984.
———. "The Politics of Poetry." $L=A=N=G=U=A=G=E$ 2.9/10 (October 1979): n. pag.
Benson, Steve. *Blindspots.* Cambridge, Mass.: Whale Cloth, 1981.
———. "For *Change." In the American Tree.* Ed. Ron Silliman. Orono, Me.: National Poetry Foundation, 1986.
———. "On Time in Another Place." Manuscript. (work in progress).
Bernstein, Charles. *Content's Dream: Essays 1975–1984.* Los Angeles: Sun & Moon, 1986.
———. *Controlling Interests.* New York: Roof, 1980.
———. *Islets/Irritations.* New York: Jordan Davies, 1983.
———, ed. "Language Sampler." *Paris Review* 86 (Winter 1982): n. pag.
Coolidge, Clark. "Arrangement." *Talking Poetics From Naropa Institute.* Ed. Anne Waldman and Marilyn Webb. Boulder: Shambhala, 1978.
———. *The Maintains.* San Francisco: This, 1974.
———. "A Note on Bop." *Code of Signals: Recent Writings in Poetics.* Ed. Michael Palmer. Berkeley: North Atlantic Books, 1983.
Grenier, Robert. *A Day at the Beach.* New York: Roof, 1984.
———. "Notes on Coolidge, Objectives, Zukofsky, Romanticism, and &." *A Symposium on Clark Coolidge.* Ed. Ron Silliman. *Stations* 5 (Winter 1978): 15–19.
———. "Typewriter vs. Typeface." Forthcoming.
Harryman, Carla. *Under the Bridge.* San Francisco: This Press, 1980.
———. "What In Fact Was Originally Improvised." *Poetics Journal* 2 (September 1982): 71–74.
Hejinian, Lyn. "The Rejection of Closure." *Writing/Talks.* Ed. Bob Perelman. Carbondale: Southern Illinois University Press, 1985.
———. "Two Stein Talks." *Temblor* 3 (1986): 128–39.
———. *"Writing Is an Aid to Memory.* Berkeley: The Figures, 1978.
Howe, Susan. *Defenestration of Prague.* New York: Kulchur, 1983.

———. *My Emily Dickinson*. Berkeley: North Atlantic Books, 1985.

Inman, P. *Ocker*. Berkeley: Tuumba, 1982.

Mac Low, Jackson. " 'Language-Centered.' " *L=A=N=G=U=A=G=E* 4 (Winter 1982): 23–26.

McCaffery, Steve. "And Who Remembers Bobby Sands?" *Poetics Journal* 5 (May 1985): 65–68.

———. "The Death of the Subject: The Implications of Counter-Communication in Recent Language-Centered Writing." *L=A=N=G=U=A=G=E* supplement one (1980): n. pag.

———, ed. *The Politics of the Referent*. In *Open Letter*, third series, 7 (Summer 1977); reprinted as *L=A=N=G=U=A=G=E* supplement one (June 1980).

Messerli, Douglas, ed. *"Language" Poetries: An Anthology*. New York: New Directions, 1987.

Palmer, Michael, ed. *Code of Signals: Recent Writings in Poetics*. Berkeley: North Atlantic Books, 1983.

———. *First Figure*. San Francisco: North Point, 1984.

———. *Notes for Echo Lake*. San Francisco: North Point, 1981.

Perelman, Bob. *a.k.a.* Berkeley: The Figures, 1982.

———. "Exchangeable Frames." *Poetics Journal* 5 (May 1985): 168–76.

———. "The First Person." *Talks*. Ed. Bob Perelman. *Hills* 6/7 (Spring 1980): 147–65.

———. *Primer*. Berkeley: This, 1981.

———. *7 Works*. Berkeley: The Figures, 1978.

———, ed. *Talks*, published as *Hills* 6/7 (Spring 1980).

———. *To the Reader*. Berkeley: Tuumba, 1984.

———, ed. *Writing/Talks*. Carbondale: Southern Illinois University Press, 1985.

Piombino, Nick. *Poems*. Los Angeles: Sun & Moon, 1988.

———. "Towards an Experiential Syntax." *Poetics Journal* 5 (May 1985): 40–51.

Robinson, Kit. *Windows*. Amherst, Mass.: Whale Cloth, 1985.

Sherry, James. "Limits of Grammar." *L=A=N=G=U=A=G=E* 4 (Winter 1982): 108–12.

———. *Popular Fiction*. New York: Roof, 1985.

Silliman, Ron. *ABC*. Berkeley: Tuumba, 1983.

———. *The Age of Huts*. New York: Roof, 1986.

———. "Demo." *Temblor* 3 (1986): 140–48.

———, ed. "The Dwelling Place: 9 Poets." *Alcheringa* 1.2 (1975): 104–20.

———. "Disappearance of the Word, Appearance of the World." *L=A=N=G=U=A=G=E* supplement three (October 1981): n. pag.

———, ed. *In the American Tree*. Orono, Me.: National Poetry Foundation, 1986.

———. *Ketjak*. San Francisco: This, 1978.

———. "Migratory Meaning: The Parsimony Principle in the Poem." *Poetics Journal* 2 (September 1982): 27–41.

———. *The New Sentence*. New York: Roof, 1987.

———. "The Political Economy of Poetry." *L=A=N=G=U=A=G=E* 4 (Winter 1982): 52–65.

———. " 'Postmodernism': Sign for a Struggle, the Struggle for the Sign." *Poetics Journal* 7 (September 1987): 18–39.

———, ed. "Realism: An Anthology of 'Language' Writing." *Ironwood* 20 (Fall 1982): 61–142.

———. "Surprised By Sign (Notes on Nine)." Ed. Ron Silliman. *Alcheringa* 1.2 (1975): 118–20.

———. *Tjanting*. Berkeley: The Figures, 1981.

———. "Ubeity." *A Symposium on Clark Coolidge*. Ed. Ron Silliman. *Stations* 5 (Winter 1978): 19–21.

Watten, Barrett. "Barrett Watten on Poetry and Politics: an Interview by George Hartley." *Sulfur* 8.3 (Winter 1988): 196–207.
———. *Complete Thought.* Berkeley: Tuumba, 1982.
———. *1–10.* San Francisco: This, 1980.
———. *Progress.* New York: Roof, 1985.
———. *Total Syntax.* Carbondale and Edwardsville: Southern Illinois University Press, 1985.
———. "The XYZ of Reading: Negativity (&)." *Poetics Journal* 6 (1986): 3–5.
Weiner, Hannah. *Clairvoyant Journal.* Lenox, Mass.: Angel Hair, 1978.

Secondary Works

Abrams, M. H. *The Mirror and the Lamp.* New York: Norton, 1958.
Adorno, Theodor. "Letters to Walter Benjamin." *Aesthetics and Politics.* Ed. Ernst Bloch. London: New Left Books, 1977.
———. *Prisms.* Cambridge, Mass.: MIT, 1981.
Allen, Donald M., ed. *The New American Poetry.* New York: Grove, 1960.
Althusser, Louis. *For Marx.* Trans. Ben Brewster. New York: Pantheon, 1969.
———. *Lenin and Philosophy.* Trans. Ben Brewster. London: New Left Books, 1971.
———, et al. *Reading Capital.* Trans. Ben Brewster. London: New Left Books, 1970.
Ashbery, John. *The Tennis Court Oath.* Middletown, Conn.: Wesleyan University Press, 1962.
Balibar, Etienne. "From Bachelard to Althusser: The Concept of the Epistemological Break." *Economy and Society* 7.3 (August 1978): 207–37.
Barthes, Roland. *Writing Degree Zero & Elements of Semiology.* Trans. Annette Lavers and Colin Smith. London: Jonathan Cape, 1984.
Bartlett, Lee. "What Is 'Language Poetry'?" *Critical Inquiry* 12.4 (Summer 1986): 741–52.
Battcock, Gregory, ed. *Minimal Art: A Critical Anthology.* New York: E. P. Dutton, 1968.
Baudrillard, Jean. *The Mirror of Production.* St. Louis: Telos, 1975.
Benjamin, Walter. "The Author as Producer." *Understanding Brecht.* Trans. Anna Bostock. London: New Left Books, 1973, pp. 85–103.
———. *Illuminations.* Ed. Hannah Arendt. New York: Schocken, 1969.
Bloch, Ernst, ed. *Aesthetics and Politics.* London: New Left Books, 1977.
Bloom, Harold, ed. *Gertrude Stein.* New York: Chelsea House, 1986.
———. "John Ashbery." *Contemporary Poetry in America.* Ed. Robert Boyers. New York: Schocken, 1974.
Brecht, Bertolt. "Against Georg Lukács." *Aesthetics and Politics.* Ed. Ernst Bloch. London: New Left Books, 1977.
Breton, André. *Selected Poems.* Trans. Kenneth White. London: Jonathan Cape, 1969.
———. *What Is Surrealism?: Selected Writings.* Ed. Franklin Rosemont. London: Pluto, 1978.
Brown, Edward J. *Mayakovsky: A Poet in the Revolution.* Princeton: Princeton University Press, 1973.
Buck-Morss, Susan. *The Origin of Negative Dialectics.* London: Free Press, 1977.
Burger, Peter. *Theory of the Avant-Garde.* Trans. Michael Shaw. Minneapolis: University of Minnesota Press, 1984.
Burn, Ian, and Mel Ramsden. *The Grammarian.* Excerpted in Meyer, Ursula, ed. *Conceptual Art.* New York: E. P. Dutton, 1972.
Coward, Rosalind, and John Ellis. *Language and Materialism.* London: Routledge & Kegan Paul, 1977.
Deleuze, Gilles, and Felix Gauttari. *Anti-Oedipus.* New York: Viking, 1977.

Derrida, Jacques. *Dissemination.* Trans. Barbara Johnson. Chicago: University of Chicago Press, 1981.

Eagleton, Terry. " 'Aesthetics and Politics.' " *New Left Review* 107 (January/February 1978): 21–34.

Ensslin, John. "Schizophrenic Writing." $L=A=N=G=U=A=G=E$ 1.4 (August 1978): n. pag.

Foster, Hall, ed. *The Anti-Aesthetic: Essays on Postmodern Culture.* Port Townsend, Wash.: Bay Press, 1983.

Greimas, A. J., and F. Rastier. "The Interaction of Semiotic Constraints." *Yale French Studies* 41 (1968): 86–105.

Jakobson, Roman. "Two Aspects of Language and Two Types of Aphasic Disturbances." *Fundamentals of Language.* S'Gravenhage: Mouton & Co., 1956.

Jameson, Fredric. *Fables of Aggression: Wyndham Lewis, the Modernist as Fascist.* Berkeley: University of California, 1979.

———. "Imaginary and Symbolic in Lacan: Marxism, Psychoanalytic Criticism, and the Problem of the Subject." *Yale French Studies* 55/56 (1977): 338–95.

———. *Marxism and Form.* Princeton: Princeton University Press, 1971.

———. *The Political Unconscious.* Ithaca: Cornell University Press, 1981.

———. "Postmodernism, or the Cultural Logic of Late Capitalism." *New Left Review* 146 (July/August 1984): 53–92.

———. *The Prison-House of Language.* Princeton: Princeton University Press, 1972.

Jay, Martin. *The Dialectical Imagination.* Boston: Little, 1973.

Kenner, Hugh. "Two Pieces on 'A.' " *Louis Zukofsky: Man and Poet.* Ed. Carroll F. Terrell. Orono, Me.: National Poetry Foundation, 1979.

Khlebnikov, Velimir. *The King of Time.* Trans. Paul Schmidt. Cambridge, Mass.: Harvard University Press, 1985.

———. *Snake Train: Poetry and Prose.* Ed. Gary Kern. Ann Arbor, Mich.: Ardis, 1976.

Krauss, Rosalind. *The Originality of the Avant-Garde and Other Modernist Myths.* Cambridge, Mass.: MIT, 1985.

Kristeva, Julia. *Revolution in Poetic Language.* Trans. Margaret Waller. New York: Columbia University Press, 1984.

Lacan, Jacques. *Ecrits.* Trans. Alan Sheridan. New York: Norton, 1977.

Laclau, Ernesto, and Chantal Mouffe. "Recasting Marxism: Hegemony and New Political Movements." *Socialist Review* 66 (November/December 1982): 91–113.

Leepa, Allen. "Minimal Art and Primary Meanings." *Minimal Art: A Critical Anthology.* Ed. Gregory Battcock. New York: E. P. Dutton, 1968.

Lemaire, Anika. *Jacques Lacan.* Trans. David Macey. London: Routledge & Kegan Paul, 1970.

Lewis, Thomas E. "Reference and Dissemination: Althusser After Derrida." *Diacritics* 15.4 (Winter 1985): 37–56.

LeWitt, Sol. "Sentences on Conceptual Art." In Lippard, Lucy. *Six Years.* New York: Praeger Publishers, 1973.

Lloyd, David. "Limits of a Language of Desire." *Poetics Journal* 5 (May 1985): 159–67.

Lukács, Georg. *History and Class Consciousness.* Trans. Rodney Livingstone. Cambridge, Mass.: MIT, 1971.

———. *Realism in Our Time.* Trans. John and Necke Mander. New York: Harper & Row, 1971.

Mandel, Ernest. *Late Capitalism.* London: New Left Books, 1978.

Marcuse, Herbert. "The Affirmative Character of Culture." *Negations.* Trans. Jeremy J. Shapiro. Boston: Beacon, 1968.

———. *One-Dimensional Man.* Boston: Beacon, 1964.

Marx, Karl. *Capital.* vol 1. New York: International, 1967.

Marx, Karl, and Friedrich Engels. *The German Ideology.* In *Marx & Engels: Basic Writings on Politics and Philosophy.* Ed. Lewis S. Feuer. Garden City, N. Y.: Anchor Books, 1959.

Merleau-Ponty, Maurice. *Signs.* Trans. Richard McCleary. Evanston, Ill.: Northwestern University Press, 1964.

Meyer, Ursula, ed. *Conceptual Art.* New York: E. P. Dutton, 1972.

Morris, Robert. "Notes on Sculpture." *Minimal Art: A Critical Anthology.* Ed. Gregory Battcock. New York: E. P. Dutton, 1968.

Motherwell, Robert, ed. *The Dada Painters and Poets: An Anthology.* 1951; rpt. Boston: G. K. Hall & Co., 1981.

Olson, Charles. *Archaeologist of Morning.* London: Cape Goliard, 1970.

———. *The Maximus Poems.* Berkeley: University of California, 1983.

———. "Projective Verse." *Human Universe.* New York: Grove, 1967.

Poulantzas, Nicos. *Political Power and Social Classes.* Trans. Timothy O'Hagan. London: New Left Books, 1973.

Richter, Hans. *Dada: Art and Anti-Art.* New York: Harry N. Abrams, 1955.

Shelley, Percy Bysshe. "A Defence of Poetry." *Shelley's Poetry and Prose: Authoritative Texts, Criticism.* Ed. Donald H. Reiman. New York: Norton, 1977.

Smithson, Robert. *The Writings of Robert Smithson.* Ed. Nancy Holt. New York: New York University Press, 1979.

Strand, Mark. *Darker: Poems.* New York: Atheneum, 1970.

Volosinov, V. N. *Marxism and the Philosophy of Language.* New York: Seminar Press, 1973.

Williams, Raymond. *Marxism and Literature.* Oxford: Oxford University Press, 1977.

Williams, William Carlos. *Imaginations.* New York: New Directions, 1970.

Wordsworth, William. *Lyrical Ballads,* 1798. Ed. W. J. B. Owen. 2nd ed. London: Oxford University Press, 1969.

Zukofsky, Louis. *"A."* Berkeley: University of California, 1978.

———. *All: The Collected Short Poems.* New York: Norton, 1971.

———. *Prepositions.* London: Rapp & Carroll, 1967.

———. "Sincerity and Objectification." *Louis Zukofsky: Man and Poet.* Ed. Carroll F. Terrell. Orono, Me.: National Poetry Foundation, 1979.

Index

Abrams, M. H., 79
Acconci, Vito, 84
Adorno, Theodor, 58–59, 61, 66, 68
Althusser, Louis, xiv, 26–31, 32, 33, 40–41, 43–45, 54, 59, 60, 61, 62
Andrews, Bruce, xi, xii, xv, 2, 4, 12–13, 23–24, 25, 39–41, 49, 53, 54, 72–78 passim, 96, 97, 98–99
Armantrout, Rae, xi
Ashbery, John, xiii, 2, 19, 23–25
Atkinson, Terry, 85

Baldwin, Michael, 85
Balibar, Etienne, 29
Ball, Hugo, 11
Barthes, Roland, 62, 77–78
Bartlett, Lee, 45
Bataille, Georges, 71
Baudrillard, Jean, 70, 71
Benjamin, Walter, 32, 56–57, 62–68 passim
Benson, Steve, xi, xiii, xv, 38–39
Benveniste, Emile, 94
Bernstein, Charles, xi, xiii, 4, 18, 24, 33, 34, 53, 75, 76, 78, 96–99 passim
Black Mountain School, xii, 19–21
Bloom, Harold, 23
Bohr, Niels, 90
Brecht, Bertolt, 53–57 passim
Breton, André, xiii, 2, 13–16, 39
Bromige, David, xi
Burger, Peter, 1, 33, 64–65
Burn, Ian, 85

Carter, Jimmy, 93
Char, René, 77
Conceptual Art, xiv, 77, 84–92, 97
Coolidge, Clark, xi, xv, 21–22, 34, 77, 80
Cubists, 6, 7

Dadaists, xiii, 7, 11–13
Davidson, Michael, 4
Davies, Alan, xi
Deleuze, Gilles, 68
Derrida, Jacques, 27, 32, 59, 62, 67, 76, 99
Dickinson, Emily, xiii, 2–4
DiPalma, Ray, xi
Duchamp, Marcel, 1, 11, 84
Dufrene, François, 69

Eagleton, Terry, 53, 75
Eco, Umberto, 31
Ensslin, John, 42

Foucault, Michel, 73
framing process, xiii, 74, 77, 83, 92–99 passim
Frankfurt School, xiv, 54, 56, 57, 59, 62, 70
Freud, Sigmund, 13, 28, 83

Gauttari, Felix, 68
Greimas, A. J., 79
Grenier, Robert, xi, xv, 5, 6, 21, 22–23, 34, 77

Harryman, Carla, xi, xii, 39, 78
Headroom, Max, 48
Hegel, Georg, 55, 58, 61, 62, 79
Heidegger, Martin, 55
Heisenberg, Werner, 90
Hejinian, Lyn, xi, xv, 5, 34, 35–36, 38, 78
Howe, Susan, xi, xii, 2–4, 98
Husserl, Edmund, 82

ideology, xiii, xiv, xv, 1, 28, 24–34 passim, 40–41, 61, 63, 73–74, 77, 92, 99
Inman, Peter, 68
Italian Futurists, 1

Jakobson, Roman, 62, 77, 94
Jameson, Frederic, xiv, 27, 32, 42–52 passim, 54, 58, 59, 60–61, 70, 71, 98
Joyce, James, 8, 55, 56, 70, 95

Kafka, Franz, 55
Kant, Immanuel, 58, 79
Kenner, Hugh, 17
Kerouac, Jack, 80
Khlebnikov, Velimir, 2, 8–10, 21, 69
Kosuth, Joseph, 86
Krauss, Rosalind, 1
Kristeva, Julia, xiii, 53, 68–69, 70
Kruchonykh, Alexei, 8–10

Lacan, Jacques, xiv, 37, 45, 46–47, 61
Laclau, Ernesto, 31
Lautreamont, Isidore Ducasse (Comte de), 11, 70
Leepa, Allen, 81
Lewis, Thomas E., 27, 29, 31–32, 34
Le Witt, Sol, 86–87
Lukács, Georg, 34, 53, 54–56, 58, 64

Mac Low, Jackson, 5, 49
Mallarmé, Stéphan, 11, 70
Mandel, Ernest, 48

Mann, Thomas, 56
Marcuse, Herbert, 33, 56, 62
Marx, Karl, 54–55, 59, 67, 69, 99
Mayakovsky, Vladimir, 2, 9–10
Mayer, Bernadette, 84
McCaffery, Steve, xi, xii, xiv, xv, 35, 49, 54, 66–72, 77, 82–84, 97, 99
Melnick, David, 10–11, 99
Merleau-Ponty, Maurice, 82
Messerli, Douglas, 89, 98
Minimalism, xiv, 77, 80–84, 85
Morris, Robert, 81
Mouffe, Chantal, 31
Musil, Robert, 55

Olson, Charles, xiii, 2, 19–21, 23

Palmer, Michael, xi, 17, 37, 93–95
Pater, Walter, 1
Perelman, Bob, xii, xv, 37–38, 42–52 passim, 88–89
Piombino, Nick, 14–16, 90
Poulantzas, Nicos, 29, 43–45, 52, 62
Poulet, Georges, 82
Pound, Ezra, 1, 19, 51

Ramsden, Mel, 85
Rastier, F., 79
reader, active vs. passive, xiii, xiv, 6, 7, 26, 27, 38, 40, 68, 81, 95
Reagan, Ronald, 62, 93
realism, xiv, 5, 34, 35–36, 53–54, 56–58, 60, 62–67, 70–76 passim
reference, xiv, 2, 31–32, 34–37, 38, 39, 76–82, 98
reification, xiv, 34–35, 39, 42, 45, 48–49, 52, 54–58, 62–69
Robinson, Kit, xii, 13, 16

Russian Formalists, 33, 62, 93
Russian Futurists, xiii, 2, 8–11, 57, 98

de Saussure, Ferdinand, 5, 31, 34, 59–60, 61, 74, 77
Seaton, Peter, xii
Sherry, James, xii, 71–72, 91–92
Silliman, Ron, xi–xv passim, 2, 6, 18, 20–21, 33, 34, 35, 45, 49, 52, 54, 59, 62–66, 69, 76, 77, 86–88, 94, 98
simulacrum, 45–46, 48–49, 71
Smithson, Robert, 89–92
Sollers, Philippe, 53
Stafford, William, 37
Stein, Gertrude, xiii, 2, 4–6, 51, 88
subject, xii, xiv, 2, 5, 26, 30–31, 34, 37, 39, 40–41, 61, 79
Surrealists, 13–16
syntax, xiii, xiv, 4, 6, 7, 12, 13, 23, 24, 33, 36, 40, 41, 51, 77–78, 80–99 passim

Tel Quel, 53, 54, 66, 75
Trotsky, Leon, 16
Tzara, Tristan, 2, 11–13

Van Gogh, Vincent, 45
Volosinov, V. N., 33

Ward, Diane, xii
Warhol, Andy, 45
Watten, Barrett, xii, xv, 16, 18, 21, 34, 39, 85–86, 91, 92–93, 96–97, 98
Weber, Max, 55
Weiner, Hannah, xii
Whitman, Walt, 2, 24
Williams, Raymond, 43
Williams, William Carlos, xiii, 2, 7–8, 19
Wordsworth, William, 79

Zukofsky, Louis, xiii, 16–18, 21, 22